How I Stopped Being a Jew

Shlomo Sand currently teaches contemporary history at the University of Tel Aviv. His books include *The Invention of the Jewish People*, *On the Nation and the Jewish People*, *The Invention of the Land of Israel*, and *Twilight of History*.

How I Stopped Being a Jew

Shlomo Sand

Translated by
David Fernbach

VERSO
London • New York

This paperback edition first published by Verso 2023
First published in English by Verso 2014
Translation © David Fernbach 2014, 2023
First published as *Comment j'ai cessé d'être juif*
© Flammarion 2013

1 3 5 7 9 10 8 6 4 2

Verso
UK: 6 Meard Street, London W1F 0EG
US: 388 Atlantic Avenue, Brooklyn, NY 11217
versobooks.com

Verso is the imprint of New Left Books

ISBN-13: 978-1-78478-200-9
ISBN-13: 978-1-78168-615-7 (US EBK)
ISBN-13: 978-1-78168-698-0 (UK EBK)

British Library Cataloguing in Publication Data
A catalogue record for this book is available from the British Library

The Library of Congress Has Cataloged the Hardback Edition as Follows:

Sand, Shlomo, author.
[Matai ve-ekh hadalti li-heyot Yehudi. English]
How I stopped being a Jew / Shlomo Sand ;
translated by David Fernbach.
     pages cm
 ISBN 978-1-78168-614-0 (hardback) – ISBN 978-1-
78168-615-7 () – ISBN 978-1-78168-698-0 ()
1. Jews–Identity. 2. National characteristics, Israeli.
3. Sand, Shlomo. 4. Judaism and state–Israel. I. Title.
DS143.S228154 2014
305.892'4–dc23

                        2014013306

Typeset in Sabon by MJ & N Gavan, Truro, Cornwall
Printed and bound by CPI Group (UK) Ltd, Croydon CR0 4YY

In memory of Eric J. Hobsbawm

In terms of suffering, I believe that the extreme human situations today are no longer Jewish ones.

– Romain Gary, 'Le judaïsme n'est pas
une question de sang', 1970

Contents

CHAPTER I

The Heart of the Matter

The main line of argument developed in this essay is bound to appear illegitimate to more than one reader, not to say repugnant. It will be rejected out of hand by many people who are determined to define themselves as Jews despite being non-religious. Others will see me simply as an infamous traitor racked by self-hatred. Consistent Judeophobes have characterized the very question of self-definition as impossible or even absurd, seeing Jews as belonging always to a different race. Both these groups maintain that a Jew is a Jew, and that there is no way a person can escape an identity given at birth. Jewishness is perceived in both cases as an immutable and monolithic essence that cannot be modified.

In the early twenty-first century, from reading newspapers, magazines and books, I do not think it exaggerated to maintain that Jews are too often presented as bearers of particular hereditary character traits or brain cells that distinguish them from other human beings, in the same way as Africans are distinguished from Europeans by their skin colour. And just as it is impossible for Africans to shed their skins, so too are Jews unable to renounce their essence.

The state of which I am a citizen, when it conducts a census of its inhabitants, defines my nationality as 'Jew', and calls itself the state of the 'Jewish people'. In other words, its founders and legislators considered this state as being the collective property of the 'Jews of the world', whether believers or not, rather than as an institutional expression of the democratic sovereignty of the body of citizens who live in it.

The State of Israel defines me as a Jew, not because I express myself in a Jewish language, hum Jewish songs, eat Jewish food, write Jewish books or carry out any Jewish activity. I am classified as a Jew because this state, after having researched my origins, has decided that I was born of a Jewish mother, herself Jewish because my grandmother was likewise, thanks to (or because of) my great-grandmother, and so on through the chain of generations until the dawn of time.

If chance should have had it that only my father was considered a Jew, while in the eyes of Israeli law my mother was 'non-Jewish', I would have been registered as an Austrian; I happen to have been born in a displaced persons camp in the town of Linz, just after the Second World War. I could indeed, in this case too, have claimed Israeli citizenship, but the fact that I spoke, swore, taught, and wrote in Hebrew, and studied throughout my youth in Israeli schools, would have been of no avail, and throughout my life I would have been considered legally as being Austrian by nationality.

Fortunately or unfortunately as the case may be, depending on how one sees this question, my mother was identified as Jewish on her arrival in Israel at the end of 1948, and the description 'Jew' was added to my identity card. Moreover, and no matter how paradoxical it might appear, according to Israeli law just as according to Judaic law (*Halakhah*), I cannot stop being a Jew. This is not within my power of free choice. My nationality could be changed in the records of the Jewish state only in the exceptional case of my conversion to another religion.

The problem is, I don't believe in a supreme being. Apart from a brief fit of mysticism at age twelve, I have always believed that man created God rather than the other way around – an invention that has always seemed to me one of the most questionable, fascinating and deadly wrought by human society. As a result, I find myself tied hand and foot, caught in the trap of my crazy identity. I don't envisage converting to Christianity, not merely because of the past cruelty of the Inquisition and the bloody Crusades, but quite simply because I don't believe in Jesus Christ, Son of God. Nor do I envisage converting to Islam, and not just on account of the traditional Sharia that allows a man, if he feels it necessary, to marry four women, whereas this privilege is refused to women. I have instead a more prosaic reason: I don't believe Muhammad was a prophet. Nor will I become a follower of Hinduism, as I disapprove of any tradition that sacralizes castes, even in an indirect and attenuated fashion. I'm even incapable of becoming a Buddhist, as I feel it impossible to transcend death and do not believe in the reincarnation of souls.

I am secular and an atheist, even if my limited brain finds it hard to grasp the infinity of the universe, given the tight and terrible limits of life here on Earth. The principles that guide my thoughts – my beliefs, if I dare use this word – have always been anthropocentric. In other words, the central place is held by human beings and not by any kind of higher power that supposedly directs them. The great religions, even the most charitable and least fanatic, are theocentric, which means that the will and designs of God stand above the lives of men, their needs, their aspirations, their dreams and their frailties.

Modern history is full of oddities and irony. Just as the ethnoreligious nationalism that emerged in the early nineteenth century forced Heinrich Heine to convert to Christianity in order to be recognized as German, and Polish nationalism in the 1930s refused to see my father as completely Polish if he would not become a Catholic, so the Zionists of the early twenty-first century, both inside and outside Israel, absolutely reject the principle of a civil Israeli nationality and recognize only a Jewish one. And this Jewish nationality can be acquired only by the almost impossible path of a religious act: all individuals who wish to see Israel as their national state must either be born of a Jewish mother, or else satisfy a long and wearisome itinerary of conversion to Judaism in conformity with the rules of Judaic law, even if they are resolutely atheist.

In the State of Israel, any definition of Jewishness is deeply deceptive, imbued with bad faith and arrogance. At the time these lines were written, a number of immigrant workers – fathers and mothers of children born and raised in Israel – applied in despair to the Chief Rabbinate to convert to Judaism, but found their request rejected out of hand. They wanted to join the 'Jewish nation' to avoid being sent back to the hell from which they'd fled, not to satisfy a belief in the Jews as a 'chosen people'.

At Tel Aviv University, I teach students of Palestinian origin. They speak a faultless Hebrew and are legally considered full Israeli citizens, yet the records of the Ministry of the Interior identify them definitively as 'Arabs', not just 'Israelis'. This mark of identity is in no way voluntary; it is imposed on them, and is almost impossible to change. You can imagine the fury that would be triggered in France, the United States, Italy, Germany or any other liberal democracy, if the authorities required that individuals who identified themselves as Jews have this attribute marked on their identity papers or that they be categorized as such in the official census of the population.

Following the Judeocide of the Second World War, the UN partition resolution of 1947 referred to the creation of a 'Jewish state', along with an adjacent 'Arab state' that never saw the light of day. It should thus be understandable why resorting to such labels at this point in the twenty-first century appears to be a questionable and dangerous anachronism. Twenty-five per cent of Israeli citizens, including the 20 per cent who are Arab, are not defined as Jews within the framework of the law. The designation 'Jew', therefore, as opposed to the designation 'Israeli', not only does not include non-Jews, but explicitly excludes them from the civic body in whose interest the state ostensibly exists. Such a restriction is not only antidemocratic; it also endangers the very existence of Israel.

The antirepublican identity policy of the State of Israel, however, is not the only motivation that compelled me to write this short essay. It does indeed occupy a key place here, and certainly contributed to the sharp assertions I have sometimes resorted to, but other factors, too, influenced the elaboration of the essay's content and objective. I wanted herein to place a large question mark against accepted ideas and assumptions that are deeply rooted, not only in the Israeli public sphere but also in the networks of globalized communication. For quite some time, I have felt a certain unease with the ways of defining Jewishness that became established within the heart of Western culture during the second half of the twentieth century and on into the twenty-first. I have the increasing impression that, in certain respects, Hitler was the victor of the Second World War. Certainly he was defeated militarily and politically, but within a few years his perverted ideology infiltrated itself and resurfaced. Today that ideology emits strong and threatening signals.

Let us not deceive ourselves. Today we are no longer threatened by the horrific Judeophobia that culminated in genocide. The morbid hatred towards Jews and their secularized descendants has not had a sudden rejuvenation in Western culture. Public and political anti-Semitism has actually retreated significantly in the liberal-democratic world.[1] Despite the shrieks of the Israeli state and its Zionist outriders in the 'diaspora', who claim that hatred of Jews, with which they equate any criticism of Israeli policy, is constantly growing, we need to

---

1. The concept of 'anti-Semitism' does occur at many points in this text, for want of a more suitable phrase. But to my mind it has dubious connotations, having been invented by Judeophobes, while the term 'Semite' is manifestly racist and lacks any historical foundation.

emphasize right away a fact that has broadly conditioned and inspired the writing of this essay.

No politician in our day can publicly make anti-Jewish statements, except perhaps in a few places in Central Europe and within the new sphere of Islamic nationalism. No serious press organ disseminates anti-Semitic twaddle, and no respectable publishing house will publish a writer, no matter how brilliant, who defends hatred of Jews. No radio station or television channel, public or private, will allow a commentator hostile to Jews to express himself or appear on-screen. And if any statements that are defamatory towards Jews should insinuate themselves into the mass media, they are quickly and effectively suppressed.

The long and tormented century of Judeophobia that the Western world experienced between approximately 1850 and 1950 has effectively ended – and just as well. It is true that a few marginal pockets of this viewpoint remain, relics handed down from the past, hatred conveyed in whispers in dubious salons or displayed in cemeteries (naturally their predestined place). This hatred is sometimes mouthed by crazed outsiders, but the broad public does not extend it the least legitimacy. To try to equate today's marginal anti-Semitism with the powerful, mainstream Judeophobia of the past amounts to greatly downplaying the impact of Jew-hatred in Western, Christian and modern civilization as expressed until the mid-twentieth century.

Yet the conception that makes Jews a 'race' with mysterious qualities, transmitted by obscure routes, still blossoms. While in former times it was a matter of simple physiological characteristics, blood, or facial shape, today it is DNA or, for the more subtle, a paler substitute: the strong belief in a direct lineage down the chain of generations. In a distant past we were dealing with a mixture of fear, contempt, hatred of the other, and ignorance. Today, on the part of the 'post-Shoah *goyim*', we face a symbiosis of fears, guilty consciences and ignorance, while among the 'new Jews' we often find victimization, narcissism, pretentiousness, and likewise a crass ignorance.

I therefore felt compelled to write the present text, as a desperate attempt to free myself from this determinist straitjacket, both blind and blinding, full of dangers for my own future and that of those dear to me. There is a close link between the identification of Jews as an *ethnos* or eternal race-people, and the politics of Israel towards those of its citizens who are viewed as non-Jews, as well as towards immigrant workers from distant lands and, clearly, towards its neighbours, deprived of rights and subject for nearly fifty years to a regime of occupation. It is hard to deny a glaring reality: the development of an essentialist, non-religious identity encourages the perpetuation of ethnocentric, racist or quasi-racist positions, both in Israel and abroad.

In light of the tragedies of the first half of the twentieth century, the emotional connection felt by Jewish descendants towards Israel is both understandable and undeniable, and it would be foolish to criticize it. However, in no way does that undeniable connection also necessitate a close connection between the conception of Jewishness as an eternal and ahistorical essence, and the growing support that a large number of those who identify themselves as Jews give to the politics of segregation that is inherent in the self-definition of the State of Israel, and to the regime of extended occupation and colonization that has been enforced in the territories conquered in 1967.

I am not writing for an audience of anti-Semites. I view them as either totally ignorant or stricken with an incurable disease. As for the more learned racists, I know no way to convince them. Instead I am writing for all those who question the origins and metamorphoses of Jewish identity, the modern forms of its existence, and the political repercussions induced by its various definitions. To this end, I shall extract certain crumbs from my patchy memory and reveal some components of the chain of personal identities I have acquired in the course of my life.

CHAPTER 2

Identity Is Not a Hat

A well-known joke will help illustrate my theoretical starting-point. In a school in the Paris suburbs, young Mohammed is seen as a little genius. Not only is he unbeatable in arithmetic, he excels in French. One fine day, the teacher comes up and asks him, 'Would you like me to call you Pierre?' The young pupil's face lights up, and he responds to this invitation with an outburst of enthusiasm. When Mohammed/Pierre arrives home later in the day, his mother says, 'Mohammed, can you go to the supermarket and get two bottles of milk?' The child replies that he's now called Pierre, and refuses to comply. In the evening his father comes back from work and asks his son to bring him some water from the fridge. The boy refuses and again demands to be called Pierre. The father gets up and slaps him, accidentally scratching the boy's face with his ring. The next morning when he arrives in the classroom, the teacher asks: 'Pierre, what's that on your face?' and the child replies, 'The Arabs beat me up!'

Clearly, this is a story told by French people and not by Arabs. Aside from what it reveals, both positive and negative, about the 'open' character of French nationality, the joke couldn't be repeated in Israel to illustrate the state's identity policy, given its segregationist dimension. That may also stimulate us to reflect a moment on the notion of identity – the self-image that it conveys, the risks of social fracture that it carries, its imaginary dimension, its evident dependence on others, and one's capacity or inability to change it.

At the risk of sounding trivial, I have to recall that very early in their existence human beings acquire an identity of their own, which demands recognition from their milieu. The 'ego' invents and sets itself an identity through permanent dialogue with the Other's regard. Even though identity as such responds to a constant and transhistorical psychological need common to all human beings, its forms and variations depend, on the one hand, on natural givens (sex, skin colour, height, and so forth), and on the other, on external – that is, social – circumstances.

Identity always proceeds from practices enacted by human individuals, and their modes of dependence on others. We bear it and cannot live without it. But even if one's identity does not always agree with other people's regard, it constitutes the point of entry for communication with them. Through it, individuals are rendered significant both to themselves and to their milieu. Their identity forms part of the definition of their status in the social body within which they evolve, interacting in turn with the identity of this body. Every individual identity, in its major traits, feeds into a collective identity, just as this latter results largely from an assemblage of particular identities and, in all probability, also of transcendent elements, both in the reciprocal relations of this collective with other groups and in its self-definition.

Beware, an identity is not a hat or an overcoat! It is possible to have several simultaneous identities; however, as distinct from hats and coats, it is hard to change them rapidly, hence the comically absurd story of little Mohammed/Pierre. A man may be an employer or an employee and, at the same time, atheist, married, tall, young, etc. These identities coexist and comprise different levels of power and hierarchy that interpenetrate and complement one another. The identity palettes of modern man, from youth to old age, constitute a fascinating subject, particularly in the way they manifest themselves in changing situations and contribute to creating – or maybe, challenging – a social order. The extreme sensitivity to attack displayed by identities of all kinds likewise constitutes an important subject that deserves discussion. Nevertheless, it is beyond my power to discuss these socio-psychological orientations in the present essay.

What I want to do here is focus on the problematic that is my main concern. If certain identities complement one another and are superimposed, others, by contrast, are mutually exclusive. It is not possible in practice to be both male and female, tall and short, married and single, and so on. In the same way, it is hard to be at the same time both Muslim and Christian, Catholic and Protestant, Buddhist and Jew, even if a few exceptional cases of syncretic and intermediate versions always turn up here and there when the initial faith begins to shatter.

Accordingly, it was impossible during the past hundred and fifty years to be at the same time French and German, Polish and Russian, Italian and Spanish, Chinese and Vietnamese, Moroccan and Algerian. Religious identity, today as in the past, and national identity, in the modern age, precisely resemble those hats and coats of which no more than one can be worn. Both religion (that is to say, monotheism rather than the polytheism that preceded it) and patriotism (excepting pre-national transition phases, situations of emigration, or post-national sensibilities) have demanded absolute exclusivity on the part of both individuals and collectives. This is a particular source of their power.

For centuries, the religious identities of the pre-modern world offered meanings and explanations for natural and social phenomena that would otherwise have remained incomprehensible. So as to overcome their finite character, they also conferred on life an aura of eternity, in the form of heaven and reincarnation. For this useful and lasting service, the various churches claimed not only financial rewards but also absolute devotion to the exclusive truth they offered.

This truth comforted believers, integrating them into a readily visible identity group, and thus gave their lives not only understanding and meaning, but also order and security. On top of his identity as peasant or blacksmith, merchant or pedlar, lord or serf, the individual knew he was also Christian, Jew, Muslim, Hindu, or Buddhist. No one was without a religious identity of some kind, just as until the recent past it was inconceivable that there should be men without a god. The expansion of the human grasp of nature, its products and its caprices, thanks to the decoding of its mysterious places and its secrets hidden in the 'essence of things', made a particular contribution to the shattering of an all-powerful god and especially to the delegitimization, in the eyes of the people, of his accredited agents on earth. The wide retreat – though not the disappearance – of traditional and institutionalized religions took place simultaneously with the growth of a new collective identity that came to assume a share of moral rule over social life. With the rise of the market economy and its apogee in industrialization and the age of imperialism, along with the powerful process of modernization of the means of human communication, from printing through radio and television, and as well with major changes in the structure of class relations, national identity came to serve as the main lightning-rod for the mental storms of the modern age.

This new collective identity became necessary for various reasons, among which we should particularly mention mobility, both horizontal (bound up with urbanization) and vertical (with social stratification), and also of course the division of labour, with its growing fragmentation, which required a homogeneous public culture to remain operational. The nation-state presided over the process of nationalization of the masses, which could not have happened without it. To this end, it drew on effective networks of public and private communication, but especially, from the late nineteenth century, on the two strong arms of compulsory education: its national-pedagogical products on the one hand, and military service with its militarist objectives on the other.

The new nationality drew widely on the earlier religious identity. It was often able to pillage its symbols and some of its rituals, which it used as foundations for the building of a new collective identity. At other times it completely secularized these, inventing new concepts, symbols and flags while still keeping them grafted onto a mythological and sometimes pagan past. Weaker than its predecessor in certain respects, particularly in the realm of the metaphysics of the soul, it asserted itself all the more boldly on other levels, particularly that of broad popular mobilization and the sentiment of being equal owners of a homeland, which it generously distributed to its supporters. The major difference between religious and national identity lies in the concept of sovereignty. For the 'authentic' religious believer, the sovereign is always outside his own personal identity, whereas for the votary of nationality, the sentiment of sovereignty is an integral part of identity. In place of the old Lord and Master of the universe, it was the nation, erected into master of its actions and responsible for its acts, that thereby became the main object of worship.

In the course of the last two centuries, national identity has solicited a total commitment of astonishing power. It has demanded that millions of men be ready to die for the defence or expansion of their homeland, while on an even greater number it has imposed a language and way of life, and imbued them with a strong sense of collective and popular solidarity unprecedented in history.

The new identity has nationalized history and adapted it to the patriotic needs of the present. The world of the national imaginary has always taken, for us, the form of a long recital.

Legends, great deeds, and the particular myths of tribes, religious communities, and kingdoms were transformed into a long, continuous narrative of imaginary peoples who had supposedly existed since the dawn of time. Misty and fragmentary images served as fictional foundations for a mythological temporal continuum, flowing since the birth of the nation.

We can certainly maintain that without the idea of the nation, history as a discipline (the teaching of which has, for many years, been how I earned my living) would not have been taught with such constancy and continuity, from primary school through to the end of secondary education. In all democracies, whether liberal or totalitarian, every pupil must recite the history of his or her 'people'. Clio, the muse of history, has become a goddess worshipped by modern peoples in order to fashion their collective identity and seal their faith in the political representation of the nation.

In the late nineteenth century, in reaction to widespread growing racialization on the part of anti-Semites, a small fraction of Jewish descendants underwent a phase of auto-nationalization, even self-racialization. This phenomenon gave new life to ancient myths and legends, and fashioned a series of secular identities of a new type. The near-disappearance of men's wearing of the kippah, tallith, and beard, and women's shaving of the head and wearing a wig, gave way in the mid-twentieth century to being 'ethnic Jews'. One segment of these new Jews became enthusiastic Zionists. Others adopted the essentialist standpoint of their detractors despite not coming to believe in a Jewish nationality.

If until a recent past, and despite all persecutions, being a Jew continued to mean worshipping a particular God, stubbornly following a host of religious commands and undertaking a series of prayers, history was now to bring surprising illusions in the field of modern identity politics. From now on, in the eyes of both anti-Semites and philo-Semites alike, a Jew would always be a Jew, but not on account of the cultural practices and norms that he or she followed. This individual would be perceived and considered a Jew not because of what he did, what he created, what he thought or what he said, but on account of an eternal and mysterious essence inherent in his personality. Indeed, Zionist scientists in Israel and elsewhere even introduce genetics. I shall try and trace some of the causes that led to this situation.

CHAPTER 3

A Secular Jewish Culture?

The start of my questioning, which like every start was not really one at all, goes back to 2001, in the spacious kitchen of an apartment in the 11th arrondissement of Paris. Michèle, the wife of one of my closest friends, surprised me on one of my visits by saying, 'Tell me, Shlomo, why is it that my husband, who never sets foot in the synagogue, does not celebrate Jewish festivals or light candles on the Sabbath, and doesn't even believe in God, is defined as a Jew, whereas no one would define me as a Christian or Catholic, given that I stopped going to church decades ago and am completely secular!'

To tell the truth, I was surprised by the direct and unexpected character of her question. I reflected on it and, as I usually do, tried to appear as though I had an answer to everything. Quite confidently, despite not being completely sure of my line of argument, I replied, 'Contrary to Christian identity, Jewish identity isn't just a matter of belief in God and a particular form of worship. History has left its mark on Jews in the form of outward signs that go beyond those of a traditional religious culture. Hostility towards them in modern times has given Jews a specific identity as victims of segregation, which has to be taken into account and respected.' The discussion naturally ended up with Hitler and Nazism, and, strong in my knowledge of history, I heaped up a pile of arguments designed to justify my friend's definition as a secular Jew, and – who knows? – perhaps also to square myself with my own identity.

Following this conversation, however, I felt a kind of diffuse unease; my own arguments had not satisfied me. Something was lacking, which I did not manage to define right away. A certain thought, which made me wary, kept insinuating itself, only to be repeatedly rejected. I worried over this for weeks without finding a way out of my obsessive questioning. As is well known, it is far easier to hold on to simple prejudices and ideas that are constantly reproduced in everyday conversation than to challenge the underlying concepts and constructions of our system of thought. As Martin Heidegger said in his time, most often in the course of our life we think less with words and concepts than they think themselves through us.

But what contradicted the idea that there are secular and atheist Jews? Hadn't there been, for millennia, a Jewish people: exiled, dispersed and wandering for two thousand years (like everyone, I still credited the Christian–Zionist myth of an 'exile of the Jewish people')? Hadn't the history of persecution thereby developed among Jews a particular sensibility, a fundamental common behaviour, a specific solidarity? Just look! Here was the secular Jewish culture in which, according to all appearances, I had grown up: didn't Karl Marx, Sigmund Freud and Albert Einstein create Jewish culture and science? Were they not, along with many others, objects of pride for the modern secular Jew? At least, that is what I so often heard on the school bench from both teachers and classmates.

The more time went on, the more my mind was troubled by this problem. There certainly was a secular Jewish culture, the proof being that people define themselves as Jews despite not believing in God and not keeping up the slightest residue of tradition. Jean-Paul Sartre's old and telling assertion that it is the anti-Semite who creates the secular Jew was still completely pertinent in my eyes. Wasn't identity fixed by the regard of the Other at least as much as by the consciousness that the subject had of himself? I continued to believe that so long as the Jew existed for the 'non-Jew' Other, it remained impossible to obliterate or abstract from 'Jewish alterity'.

And yet, when I began honestly to sort out what exactly constituted a secular Jewish culture, the difficulty of formulating such a definition suddenly came home to me, and I found myself plunged in an abyss of perplexity. Assuredly there is an ancestral religious culture, with its folkloric and exotic appurtenances. The Bible, far from being solely the property of Judaism, constitutes one of the cultural and historical foundations of all Western monotheistic religions (Judaism, Christianity and Islam), but the Mishnah and Talmud, Saadia Gaon, Maimonides and the other rabbinical exegetes – these were Jewish creations and creators par excellence. There has also been a major line of Jewish thought in the modern age. In the wake of Moses Mendelssohn, Hermann Cohen, Franz Rosenzweig, Martin Buber, Abraham Joshua Heschel and through to Emmanuel Levinas, various thinkers have sought to gloss and advance a Jewish philosophical reflection, a field in which they have succeeded, here and there, in obtaining significant results – though it must be mentioned that, for all its originality, this thought is always nourished by non-Jewish philosophical syntheses.[1]

What, then, is the specific culture shared by those who define themselves as secular and atheist Jews? Do they have a common language, with both élitist and popular expressions? Isn't the culture of a people characterized above all

---

1. I do not include Spinoza in this list. The contemptible practice, in Israel and elsewhere, of presenting him as a Jewish thinker rather than simply a philosopher from a Jewish background reveals the essentialist and tribalist conceptions of those who call themselves 'secular Jews'. Not only was Spinoza ostracized and his works banned in his lifetime by the Jewish community, but he himself, in his maturity, no longer saw himself as a Jew and always spoke of Jews in the third person. And despite having been given at birth the Hebrew first name Baruch, he never used it, always writing his name as Benedict or Benedictus.

by their spoken language, and in particular by their recourse to specific codes through which communication is effected? What way of life distinguishes and characterizes secular Jews? Where are Jewish plays or films produced nowadays? Why is there no secular Jewish poetry, literature or philosophy? Are there ways of being, gestures and tastes that are specific and common to all the Jews of the world, or at least to a majority of them? In other words, is there a creative Jewish culture that serves as spiritual nourishment or everyday expression for those people in the world who are identified as Jews? Can one genuinely point to Jewish elements in the work of Karl Marx, Sigmund Freud or Albert Einstein? Has the critique of capitalism, the theory of the unconscious, or the theory of relativity contributed in some way to preserving and shaping a secular Jewish culture?

Knowing that each of these questions calls for a negative answer, I understood that my secular Jewish identity was based simply on my origin, that is, exclusively on the past or, more exactly, on my reconstructed memory of it. The present and future scarcely came into play in the collective Jewish identity I had sought to justify as a living identity, supported by a specific culture. Nowhere to be found is there a way of life common to all so-called secular Jews. They do not experience today pains or joys shared by other secular Jews the world over. They do not communicate or dream in a language specific to themselves: instead they express themselves, earn their living, cry and believe, each in their own respective national language and culture.

Tristan Tzara, né Samuel Rosenstock, whose Dadaist rebellion lit up my own youth, did not write Jewish poetry. Harold Pinter, of Eastern European Jewish origin, a playwright and scriptwriter whose work has always enchanted me, produced masterpieces in English that have nothing Jewish about them. Stanley Kubrick, my favourite film director, made films that are both very American and very universal, but without an ounce of Jewishness. Henri Bergson, the philosopher with whose concept of time I had to grapple while writing my doctoral thesis, did not present to the world a Jewish philosophy. Marc Bloch, one of the greatest of twentieth-century historians, from whom I sought in vain to steal lines of argument and narrative techniques, had no interest at all in Jewish history but was completely immersed in the history of Europe. Was Arthur Koestler, a bold provocateur who helped me greatly in the shedding of my Communist illusions, a Jewish writer? And could it be that Serge Gainsbourg, whom I've admired for so long, composed and interpreted Jewish songs and not French songs without anyone noticing?

All the above-mentioned individuals, and far more, came from a Jewish family background of one sort or another. It is true that, indirectly, this background may help explain the presence of a relatively large number of individuals of Jewish origin in the fields of Western science and culture. The situation of protracted marginality of a persecuted religious minority, restricted against its will to spheres of abstract activity, formed a springboard for rapid accession to and success in the modern world, marked as this world has been by the growing production of signs and symbols.

Indeed, in some cultural creators, there are fragments from a Jewish past already in the throes of dissolution, fragments that may be called 'post-Jewish'. Although he tried to learn Hebrew at a certain point in his life, Franz Kafka produced a body of work that is manifestly not Jewish, and in which, quite deliberately, he did not put a single Jewish character. We may infer, all the same, that the life led by his family in Central Europe probably helped give rise to the strong expression of signs of alienation and anxiety in his stories. This is true likewise of Walter Benjamin: his curiosity about the milieu of Jewish origin from which he came led him to interest himself for a while in Hebrew and in the mysticism of the Kabbalah, from which, however, he soon took his distance in order to immerse himself completely in the critique of German culture – more correctly, in fact, European culture, as witnessed in his highly original writings on France. In his work, too, one finds expressed a tragic dimension whose roots tap into his Jewish family background as well as other sources.

It is also true that a share of Eastern European sensibility, both Jewish and specifically Yiddish, resonates strongly in the works of Stefan Zweig, Joseph Roth, Irène Némirovsky, Saul Bellow, Philip Roth, Henry Roth and Chaim Potok, among many others. But Philip Roth, for example, who is sometimes accused of anti-Semitism, insisted more than once that he wrote as an American, not as a Jew, and it is clear that the characters of Yiddish origin who feature in his novels are the last Mohicans of a disappearing generation.

None of these authors created any secular culture common to all Jewish descendants, nor even to a majority of their number. Even a novice anthropologist knows that a culture and a sensibility do not have their source merely in the legacy of ancestors, nor only in the signs and traces left by memory, but are constructed above all on shared experience, on modes of communication, and on the interactions and contradictions of lived reality. Knowing that there is no specific mode of everyday life that could bind together secular individuals of Jewish origin across the world, it is impossible to assert the existence either of a living, non-religious Jewish culture or of a possible common future, apart from vestiges handed down from a declining religious tradition.

Again, it is incontestable that many secular people of Jewish origin, despite being totally atheist, continue to celebrate certain festivals and ceremonies that issue from the long history of Jewish cultural practices. Some teach their children to light a Hanukkah candle for the winter Feast of

Lights, others to participate in the Pesach (Passover), Seder in the spring or even to attend synagogue in autumn on Yom Kippur, the Day of Atonement. But then, should we designate as Christians the secular French or German atheists who celebrate the birth of Jesus, put up a pine tree in their living-room, and place presents for their children beneath it? And as for the American agnostics of Jewish origin who hang an eight-branched candlestick on their Christmas tree, should we call them Judeo-Christians? Theodor Herzl, for example, the founder of political Zionism in the late nineteenth century, did not have his son circumcised and used to celebrate Hanukkah with a Christmas tree; on the basis of those practices, should we call him a Christian or a Jew? Perhaps he was 'a bit' Christian, and was led to change his identity and become a 'new Jew' under the influence of a hostile environment.

Whereas synagogues, churches and mosques are viewed by nonbelievers as museums of a kind, it would appear that festivals, commemorations and ceremonies, on the other hand, are cultural signs charged with a significance whose value does not disappear and which it is not easy to abandon. They break the uniformity of the cycle of days; they return us for a moment to families that may tend to drift or even break apart; they bring back nostalgic memories of the dear departed. But no culture can be reduced to nostalgia and ritual commemorations of a religious origin; although these may well constitute a significant point of departure in the complex system of self-definition, they also risk contributing to the erection of dividing walls between people. If young people are prevented, in the name of a religious tradition, from meeting and loving, and if faith and the respect for beliefs, or the fears of relatives, incite people to reject and devalorize those who are deemed different from themselves, they are then condemned to remain imprisoned throughout life to these points of departure that have ossified over time, and that soon distort and even threaten. National societies in which religious–communitarian criteria play a dominant role in the dividing lines of identity cannot be described as liberal or democratic.

As a result, I became increasingly vexed by the disturbing question of whether my secular Jewish identity had in fact been based on anything more than a dead past. Certainly, from the point of view of a living present called on to create and orient the future, it was hollow. What is this past, and what is its history? The geological strata that surround and overlie these questions play a significant role in understanding the identitarian development of those who define themselves as Jews. I shall now try to cast some unsteady and fragmentary beams of light on these retrospective Jewish and Zionist constructions.

CHAPTER 4

Pain and Duration

In 1975 I arrived in France to pursue my study of history. That same year, my father, who had lived continuously in Israel since 1948, left the country for the first time to visit his brother in Montreal. He stopped off en route to meet me in Paris. I was proud to be able to act as his guide in the 'city of light', and I recall that we were lucky enough to enjoy warm and sunny weather, with golden sunsets illuminating the monuments and roofs of the city.

While we were strolling, my father said that he could recognize a Jew in the street. 'You always complain of living with too many Jews in Israel,' I said to him, 'surely you've not come to Paris to look for more! And besides, how could you prove that the person you identify really is a Jew?'

Soon afterwards, at a bus stop, there was a tall man standing next to us in line; he had grey hair and blue eyes, and looked to me like just another old man. My father whispered in my ear that he actually was a Jew, and to prove it, said that we should speak Yiddish, on the assumption that the unknown man would then join our conservation. As two Israelis, or two 'typical' Mediterraneans, it wasn't hard for us to make a noise. The Jewish 'target' took no notice and didn't even turn towards us.

During the bus ride, my father asked me about every square, every crossroads, every monument we passed. When we reached a certain point, I think it was Place Vendôme, he asked me the name of the column standing in the middle. Despite my fairly good knowledge of Paris, I found myself unable to answer. Suddenly the man my father had identified as a Jew, who was sitting in front of us, turned round and began to explain in Yiddish the origin of the column. It turned out that he came from Romania and had arrived in France before the Second World War. He was an engineer and lived in Montmartre.

I was flabbergasted and speechless. When we got off the bus, I immediately asked my father how he'd been able to identity this man. 'It's because of the eyes,' he replied. I found this hard to understand. 'But he had blue eyes!' I said. 'It's not the shape or the colour, it's the look.' 'What look?' 'A fleeting and sad look, the mark of fear and deep apprehension,' explained my father. 'That's how the German soldiers sometimes identified Jews in Poland. But don't worry, you don't get that anymore with young Israelis!'

And so I then examined my father's look very closely, as never before, and it seemed that for the first time I perceived the impact that a situation of prolonged marginality could have on someone's mentality. It's almost unnecessary to add that, given my native Israeli impatience, I had not previously paid this the slightest attention.

A history of suffering, a history of persecution, a history of a minority group's resistance in the midst of a hostile and dominant religious civilization: the story told by the eyes is far too long to be conveyed in the context of this short essay. And yet, before readers conclude that they are reading yet another tale of Jewish victimization, intended to arouse in the *goyim* a feeling of guilt and so accumulate additional moral capital of commiseration, I must add a few small, unkind comments.

I have always avoided wallowing in the invocation of past sufferings, and never dreamed of repairing the misfortunes of yesterday. My own place is among those who try to discern and root out, or at least reduce, the excessive injustices of the here-and-now. The persecuted and victimized of yesterday seem to me less a matter of priority than the persecuted of today or the victimized of tomorrow. I also know how history serves only too often as an arena in which the roles of hunter and hunted, strong and weak, are shuffled around.

As a scholar and teacher of history, I am aware that Jews have not always and everywhere suffered persecution and, where they have, it has not been with the same violence or frequency. The existences of the Jews of Babylon in the Persian and Hellenic ages, the Jews of the great convert kingdoms, the Jews of Muslim Andalusia and other communities throughout history have been varied, and it is impossible to speak of a common destiny. Moreover, in places where Jews ruled, such as the Hasmonean kingdom of the second century BCE or the Himyarite kingdom during the fifth century CE in the Arabian Peninsula, their behaviour towards others was precisely similar to what they themselves experienced elsewhere and subsequently. It is incontestable, however, that in medieval Europe, and especially in the east of the continent on the threshold of the modern age, millions of Jews endured alienation and lived as foreigners, in a deep and lasting insecurity which can be neither forgotten nor relativized.

In order to understand all this, we need to go back through the tunnel of time to distant eras, shrouded in indistinctness and fog, which often makes them hard to situate. Originally, we find a monotheistic belief that it is still difficult to define as Jewish and would be more correct to call Yahwistic. This began to take shape in the fifth century BCE, sometime after the political and clerical élite of Jerusalem were exiled by Babylon. The majority of the admirable stories of the Bible were composed under the effects of this unprecedented disruption as well as the encounter with Persian Zoroastrianism. In the second century BCE, the young religion was already sufficiently sure of itself to rise up and establish in Judea the

first theocratic and monotheistic kingdom, which would for-
cibly convert all its own subjects and those of neighbouring
lands.

The revolutionary new faith erupted and spread by way of
Hellenistic cultural networks and then via Roman communication routes around the Mediterranean. After the defeat of
its three great revolts against paganism, during the late first
and early second centuries CE, it split into two major currents,
with an ever-growing gulf between them: rabbinical Judaism
and Pauline Christianity. The former, less powerful, gave the
world the Mishnah and Talmud. The latter, stronger and more
effective, brought forth the New Testament. Christianity was
easily the victor, and imposed on its defeated competitor a
long and painful historical state of siege.

Contrary to accepted ideas, Jewish self-enclosure was not the
result of Judaic dogma, even if this dogma had, from its origins,
conveyed the principle of exclusion, as testified by several
books of the Old Testament. Certainly, the early Yahwistic
monotheism appeared fearful and unsure of itself, but as it
grew it gained strength, and exponents of its Judaic variant
embarked on an offensive and effective proselytism, giving
rise, it would seem, to the majority of the world's Jewish communities. Only the threat posed by Christianity, and later by
Islam, reactivated its sectarian foundations, so that its autarkic
self-enclosure resulted above all from its attempts to survive in
the face of a permanent existential threat. With the triumph of
Christianity, in the fourth century, law and power forced Jews
to retrench behind the gates of their faith. This was the end of
the great wave of Judaization which had travelled the entire
Mediterranean, and Jewish missionary activity from then on
would be confined to the margins of medieval Christian civilization. It suffered a second blow with the rise of Islam, its other
younger sister, and subsequently found itself once again subject
to the goodwill and good humour of other powers.

At this juncture, it may be useful to mention a historical fact that arouses a certain awkwardness among all those who take pride today in belonging to 'Judeo-Christian' civilization. The fate of Jewish communities in the shadow of Islam was very different from the often dark fate they experienced in Europe. True, Islam saw Judaism as an inferior religion, and cases of persecution did occur. But on the whole, the Muslims granted Judaism the respect due to an ancient divine faith that, like Christianity, needed to be sheltered and protected by the dominant religion.

Jews were called in the Koran 'People of the Book' (sura 9:5), whereas in the much earlier New Testament, it was said of them: 'They will fall at the sword's point; they will be carried captive into all countries' (Luke 21:24). Following the accounts of the Gospels, the Jews were generally regarded in the Christian world as descendants of the murderers of Jesus, expelled from Jerusalem by force. During most of its phases, and for a substantial portion of its temporal and spiritual descendants, Christianity refused to see Judaism as a legitimate competing religion. There was only one true Israel (*verus Israel*) – not two, and certainly not three! Christianity rejected in principle the possibility that a different monotheism, Jewish or Muslim, might exist alongside it. By the end of the Middle Ages, not a single Muslim community remained in Europe, whereas Christian communities continued their existence in the lands of Islam.

For Christianity, it was both incomprehensible and unacceptable that Jews could voluntarily remain faithful to another religion and refuse to recognize that grace had already come to earth in the form of the Messiah. Thus, in the Christian imagination, Jews remained the scions of Judas Iscariot, who had been banished from Jerusalem because of their sins, and they continued to appear as a threat to the faithful in Christ, themselves pure and innocent. In contrast to what pagans sometimes experienced, the Church made no plans for the extermination of the Jews; instead it chose to preserve the wretched Jew as proof of the rightness of the path taken by the true faith. But prejudices, periodic offensives, mass expulsions, accusations of ritual crime, and spontaneous pogroms did form an integral part of 'Judeo-Christian' civilization from its origins to the threshold of the modern age.

This religious hatred of the Other, of long duration, formed the conceptual basis for the emergence of modern Judeophobia in the nineteenth century. Without this extended background, the new nationalist and racist hatred would in all likelihood not have risen into such a torrent or enjoyed such wide distribution. Besides, if in principle, until that time and despite all obstacles, Jews had been able to 'improve' themselves and 'make amends' by converting to Christianity at the cost of great effort and goodwill, now the path of salvation offered by the repudiation of their traditional faith would be blocked. Jews would be unable to become true Anglo-Saxons, proud Gallo-Catholics, genuine Teutonic Aryans or authentic indigenous Slavs.

When Jewish believers began to emancipate themselves en masse from the very real ghettos imposed on them for so long by Christian powers, but also from the ideological and mental ghetto built by Jewish cultural institutions, and began to take an active part in the creation of national cultures in Europe, there was born in parallel with this an aggressive racism that rejected them. While their quite common situation of living in urban communities had predisposed Jews and their descendants (whether of Judaic faith or completely secular) to appear in cultural and linguistic terms just like the earlier French, Germans, Dutch or British, modern nationalism constantly presented them as a foreign body secretly developing in the arteries of – and ever ready to sink their hooks into – the new nations.

In the great process of national construction, the French certainly needed the German enemy, the Germans the Slav enemy, the Poles the Orthodox enemy, and so on. The Jews, however, in their role of *longue durée* enemy, remained irreplaceable and highly effective as a foil to the ethnocentric crystallization of nations erected on a Christian foundation.

To constitute itself, the fictional invention of a common national origin needed every inch and every cultural spark of unity, whether linguistic or religious. Jewishness, as the antithesis of Christianness, effectively fulfilled this function, although there were certainly local differences: Judeophobia had freer rein in Paris than in London, in Berlin than in Paris, in Vienna than in Berlin, and in Budapest, Warsaw, Kiev or Minsk than in the West. Almost everywhere, the emerging nationalism took from the existing Christian tradition the deicidal Jew and grafted it onto the figure of the foreign Other, the better to mark the boundaries of the new nation. To be sure, the spokesmen of these nations were not all Judeophobes, but all political anti-Semites presented themselves as zealous prophets of nation-building.

The long century of Judeophobia, as previously noted, ran from 1850 to 1950. 'Judaism in Music', Richard Wagner's famous article first published in 1850, could be taken as its symbolic official date of birth, while the suppression by Pope John XXIII in 1959 of the description of the Jews as heretical and traitorous (*perfidis*) marked its end. The recrudescence of modern hatred, culminating with meteoric speed in the advent of the Nazi monster, took place against the background of an increase in the flow of Jewish emigration from Eastern Europe in the late nineteenth century. Just as hostility towards Arab and Muslim immigrants in our own day contributes to characterizing, specifying and sharpening Europe's 'white' and 'Judeo-Christian' identity, constructed not without effort and difficulty, so too have the waves of immigration of Yiddish populations had the effect in their time of crystallizing ethnonational awareness. These immigrants came from places where Jews lived in a situation of far greater distress than anywhere in the West, or indeed in the Islamic world.

CHAPTER 5

Immigration and Judeophobia

A few years after completing my doctoral thesis on the sulphurous philosopher Georges Sorel, my research interest turned to one of his friends, who deserves to be seen as among the most curious intellectual figures of the turn of the century. With rare bravura, and in opposition to his entire milieu, Bernard Lazare was in fact the first person to rouse himself to prove the innocence of Alfred Dreyfus. His battle, and his nonconformist spirit, led him to become proudly outspoken as a Jew. A self-definition of this kind was in no way acceptable or popular at that time among 'Israelite' milieus in Western and Central Europe.[1]

Despite not making Palestine the land of his dreams, Bernard Lazare may be considered the first French Zionist, as he formulated the Jewish right to national self-determination. He resigned from the Zionist movement after Theodor Herzl and his supporters, in order to advance their plans, refused to denounce the repression of the Armenians by the Ottoman sultan, deeming it a greater priority to establish a bank to finance colonization in the Holy Land. Yet until his dying day Lazare continued his struggle in support of Jewish victims of oppression in Romania, devoting to this the greater part of his scant forces and resources until his death in 1903.

It is less well known, however, that at the dawn of his career,

---

1. In the nineteenth century, several Jewish institutions and milieus in Western and Central Europe came to prefer the term 'Israelite', on account of the negative connotation that 'Jew' had in the long Christian tradition.

in the early 1890s, this symbolist poet and anarchist publicist was partly anti-Semitic, in the sense that his practice was to attack not all Jews but only 'Oriental' ones. In cutting articles, he argued that the elegant and refined Portuguese and Spanish ('Sephardic') Israelites, in whom he recognized himself, should not be equated with the Jewish *epigoni* from the tribes of the Huns, dirty and ugly, who were steadily arriving in considerable numbers from the Tsarist empire. In accordance with the fashion of the time, Lazare was persuaded that the latter constituted a distinct race, with a totally different origin from that of the Jews of Central Europe. He was equally of the view that their immigration into France and neighbouring countries should be prevented at all costs.

This point of view on the part of a French intellectual, radical though it was, was in no way exceptional. It was, in fact, more or less the view of the so-called Gallo-Catholics, Anglo-Saxons, Aryan Germans and many others concerning the threats posed by immigration to the 'autochthonous' cultures of the West. The cultivated Israelite communities of Paris, London and Berlin thought no differently.

At the end of the nineteenth century, about 80 per cent of the world's Jews and their secular descendants, that is, more than seven million individuals, lived in the Russian empire, Austro-Hungarian Galicia, and Romania (in addition, a more than negligible proportion of German Jews hailed from Eastern Europe). This surprising demographic phenomenon is not explained by a supposed abundance of food that the Jews had cunningly managed to appropriate at the expense of their neighbours. Nor is the explanation to be sought in the indefatigable sexuality of Jewish males, as anti-Semites of the day likewise imagined, nor by the fact that Jews washed their hands before eating – though Zionist historians have sometimes proposed that curious argument. There was no demographic explosion among the Jews of Western Europe, who also washed their hands before eating, but lived in a situation of relative prosperity, at least when compared with those of the East. The same was true even in North Africa and the Middle East, where Jews generally endured less threatening pressures from their Muslim neighbours.

Until the late 1960s, the majority of historians of Judaism, whether Zionist or not, championed the hypothesis that only the existence of the medieval Jewish Khazar kingdom – on the steppes of southern Russia, eastern Ukraine and the Caucasus – could have generated such surprising demographic growth, perhaps the most significant in modern Jewish history. The weakening and subsequent breakup of this kingdom, between the tenth and twelfth centuries, led to the migration of Jews to the West, to those lands that would become western Ukraine, Lithuania, Poland, Belarus, Galicia, Hungary and Romania. (In the mid-eighteenth century, shortly before the start of the large upsurge in the European population, there were more than 750,000 Jews in the kingdom of Poland and Lithuania alone, as against only 150,000 in Western Europe.)

As distinct from other Jewish communities across the world, the Jewish population of Eastern Europe had preserved ways of life and culture that were completely different from those of their non-Jewish neighbours. In France, Italy, western Germany, the Iberian Peninsula, North Africa and the northern reaches of the Fertile Crescent, the Jews, whether converted indigenous people or immigrants, shared both language and the everyday habits of life with their neighbours; settlements were almost always shared by both, whereas Eastern Europe underwent a very different sociocultural development.

The Jews of Eastern Europe were grouped for centuries into separate townships or other localities, in which they formed a majority or at least a large minority. The Jewish *shtetl*, half rural and half urban, formed the principal cradle of the vast

Yiddish population. With the beginnings of urbanization, they preserved their cultural specificity not only in practising the same religion as Jews in other parts of the world, but also in their 'secular' everyday life. They ate kosher food but also developed culinary habits different from those of their non-Jewish neighbours. They wore the kippah but also fur hats, and dressed in a fashion distinct from that adopted by the surrounding mass of peasants. They hardly spoke the language of their neighbours; instead, in their working life and in their function as intermediaries, they preferred to resort to the Germanic dialects widely used in economic transactions. The arrival of learned German-speaking rabbis also influenced the formation of specific Yiddish idioms, with a more Slavic inflection in the eastern regions and a more Germanic one in the western.

We should also emphasize that, as distinct from the small Jewish communities of Western Europe or the Islamic world, which had adopted flexible and relatively symbolic religious customs, the Yiddish speakers of Eastern Europe maintained rigid practices of worship that strikingly marked their difference from their non-Jewish neighbours and environment. In many respects, this form of religious fundamentalism exhibited an affinity with the strictest currents of Orthodox Christianity (and a certain closeness may be noted between Hassidic mysticism and the popular Christian mysticism of these regions). With the onset of modernization and secularization, this world of intransigent commands led a certain number of secularized heirs of these Jewish families to adopt an attitude of marked hostility towards a religious tradition so closed in on itself. Many Jewish sons and daughters thus became atheist socialists (Socialist Revolutionaries, Mensheviks, Bolsheviks, Bundists, anarchists, and so on). The response of the religious authorities was similarly hostile, rejecting all connection with these apostates.

Like its Austro-Hungarian counterpart, the Russian empire was far too large and backward to provide a state springboard for the birth of a united nationality that would bring people together on a civil basis, following the model already undertaken in the major countries of Western Europe. In the hands of the tsarist power, Pan-Slavic nationalism served, above all, as an instrument of manipulation and oppression. This is why local and fragmented national components appeared, both within Pan-Slavism and against it, owing to the plurality of languages and religions. Poles, Ukrainians, Lithuanians, Latvians and so on all came into being in this way. In almost all regions inhabited by mixed populations that spoke different dialects, intolerable and dangerous conflicts appeared. But it was the presence of the Yiddish population in these areas that had the effect of escalating the modern intolerance so characteristic of all ethnocentric nationalist currents. The wave of pogroms that began in the 1880s, at the same time as the restrictions imposed by the tsar and in particular the insufferable living conditions in the Pale of Settlement, started to propel Jewish communities outward, in a flow of emigration that spilled into Vienna, Berlin, London, New York and Buenos Aires.

Estimates of the size of this migration vary. But at least three million people were uprooted and cast on the roads between the 1880s and the Second World War. This great mass moved rapidly westward, arousing, as we have seen, strong reactions of hostility and fear, not only among the non-Jewish public but equally on the part of European Jewish institutions. These displaced immigrants, with their strange dress, peculiar customs and particular language, gathered in the capitals of Central and Western Europe, while many ended up reaching the Americas, both North and South.

The rise of Judeophobia, and its relation with this wave of migration, has thus far scarcely been addressed by serious research on a Europe-wide scale. Nonetheless, investigations meant to explain the long and painful experience that led to the Nazi genocide must involve not only attempts to decipher the ethnocentric, Judeophobic currents that were widespread in Europe, not only analysis of the specific character of German nationalism, not simply an understanding of the crystallization and specific character of the Nazi state apparatus or a deeper decoding of the paths by which the systemic violence of the First World War made possible the industrialized crime of the Second. These investigations must also include a rigorous analysis of the thresholds of sensitivity and hostility that were breached during this great upheaval of populations.

The pogroms and uprooting were the first blow dealt to the Yiddish people who had began to take shape and unity in the wake of the modernization process of the late nineteenth century. The second blow came from the Bolshevik Revolution, which sought to stifle the varied expressions of this particular culture through administrative measures. The third and moral blow was delivered by the Nazis, who perpetrated the physical extermination of the majority of the Jews who remained in Europe. Zionism dealt a fourth blow, in working to wipe out Yiddish linguistic and cultural practices. This is not, of course, to place all these events on the same level, either in terms of their motivations or their results, and still less so in terms of their morality.

CHAPTER 6

From One Oriental to Another

In 1971 I was accepted as a student at Tel Aviv University. Since my level of English was inadequate, I was forced to take a remediation course. At the first lecture, when I was still tormented by the fear of failure, the English professor asked the students to note on a sheet of paper all the languages besides Hebrew that they spoke. At the start of the second lecture, the teacher asked, 'Who is Shlomo Sand?' I raised a finger, not without trepidation, fearing I was about to undergo a repeat of the nightmare I had experienced at secondary school before being expelled. But this was a different story: 'Sand is the only one to have mentioned Yiddish,' he said. 'Who else in the class speaks Yiddish?' Nine hands went up. It was evident that, in the early 1970s, there were still many who dared not admit that they spoke the wretched 'language of exile'. To tell the truth, I was a little ashamed myself, and hesitated a while before noting Yiddish as a second language of mine.

In fact, it wasn't even second. Yiddish had actually been my mother tongue; it was in Yiddish that I spoke with my parents, beginning with the first words that came out of my mouth. With the death of my parents and their intimates, I no longer had anyone with whom I could speak Yiddish, and so the language of my childhood slipped into the folds of my subconscious or began to fade altogether. It was in Paris, meeting former Bundists or Communists – of whom I met still more during my first visit to New York, in 1998 – that I became more broadly acquainted with the survivors of the Yiddish population that was in the process of disappearing. It was the last period of my life when I could practise the language of the old immigrants from Eastern Europe, whereas in Israel the majority of them refrained from speaking Yiddish in public places (other than in Hasidic schools, which I never attended).

It was also after that first stay in the United States that I understood why Americans equate and confuse Yiddish identity with a general imaginary Jewish identity. They cannot distinguish between, on the one hand, a popular culture that prospered within a large population in a large though limited territory, and a religious culture spread across every continent in varying forms. What is called 'Jewish humour', for example, is actually Yiddish–Slavic humour (to use Romain Gary's expression) and continues to fuel New York jokes and the films of Woody Allen. This particularly inspired both Nikolai Gogol and Sholem Aleichem, but neither the Rothschilds nor the marvellous Judeo-Iraqi writers ever shared it, using other canons of comedy for the purpose of inducing laughter. Contemporary Israeli humour is also totally different – a cultural expression flowing directly from geography, in other words, from modes of everyday life rather than a higher written tradition, and including a wide vocabulary of insults and oaths.

The rich Yiddish culture is now extinct. It is true that some students take classes in the language of the Eastern European Jews, but they do not communicate or create in this language. Linguistic study and the connection with Yiddish culture may warm the hearts of nostalgists, but they cannot possibly create characters and situations like those encountered in the literary monuments bequeathed by such writers as Sholem Aleichem or Isaac Bashevis Singer. (It is no accident, by the way, that these two giants of Yiddish literature both ended their lives in North America, not in the Middle East.) Another disappearance was the fine dream of the Bund, the great Jewish social democratic party of the Russian empire, subsequently of Poland, which, contrary to Zionism, was based on a living popular culture and so had no need to dress itself up in religious guise in order to constitute a semi-national class identity.

The number of persons who spoke the various dialects of Yiddish on the eve of the Second World War is estimated to be more than ten million; in the early twenty-first century there are no more than a few hundred thousand, chiefly among the Haredim, the strictly Orthodox 'God-fearers'. A popular culture has completely disappeared, wiped out without any hope of resuscitation, as it is truly impossible to bring back to life a culture or a language. The presumption that Zionism can resuscitate ancient Hebrew and the culture of the 'people of the Bible' is based on no more than a mythical quest for national references – a belief on which generations of Israelis and Zionists across the world have been brought up, leading them to believe in its truth.

If the first theorists of the Zionist idea included many of German cultural background, the founders of the colonizing enterprise had instead been immersed in the Yiddish culture of Eastern Europe; their mother tongue was that 'minor jargon' caricatured by German Israelites, that is to say, by the Ashkenazim. The Yiddish colonists, in fact, were very quick to discard their despised mother tongue. The first thing they needed was a language that could unite Jews the world over, and neither Theodor Herzl nor Edmond de Rothschild could communicate in Yiddish. The early Zionists subsequently aspired to create a new Jew, who would break with the popular culture of their parents and ancestors as well as with the wretched townships of the Pale of Settlement.

Starting from earlier attempts, made in the Russian empire, that sought to adapt biblical texts and prayers into a modern language, Zionist linguists set out to create a new language of communication whose principal lexicon was indeed drawn from the books of the Bible but whose writing was Aramaic and Assyrian (that is, taken from the Mishnah, rather than being Hebraic), with a syntax predominantly Yiddish and Slavic, and thus in no way biblical. This language today is incorrectly called 'Hebrew' (I myself am forced to call it that, for want of anything better), but it would be far more appropriate to follow the lead of progressive linguists and define it as 'Israeli'.

This new language developed well before the founding of the State of Israel, rapidly becoming the language of official communication used by the Zionist community that settled in Palestine. It became the spoken and written language of the children of these pioneers, who would subsequently form the cultural, military and political élite of the early Israeli state. These 'Sabras' expressed a firm and vigorous rejection of Yiddish culture, an attitude which they were strongly encouraged to adopt by the leaders of the immigrant community. David Ben-Gurion had banned the use of the language of the Eastern European Jews in the congresses of his socialist party, and at least one situation has gone down in legend, when a former fighter with the Vilnius partisans, speaking in 1944 at a Histadrut meeting about the extermination of Jews in her country, had her speech interrupted by Ben-Gurion himself, who came to the tribune to condemn this use of a 'shrill foreign tongue'.

The Hebrew University of Jerusalem, which officially opened its doors in 1925, did not have a chair in Yiddish, and students who wished to study the destroyed culture had to wait until 1951 to do so. In 1949, just after the creation of the State of Israel, with the massive arrival of Yiddish-speaking survivors of the genocide, a law was passed that prohibited Israeli citizens from staging public performances in the language of these immigrants (only invited foreign artists had the right to express themselves in the language of 'exile', but for periods not exceeding six weeks). Not until the early 1970s, when the complete victory of the new autochthonic culture was assured, could the position towards the despised language be softened.

This disdain and discredit of Yiddish did not signal a preference for, or a more flexible attitude towards, the culture and language of other immigrant communities. In the utopian vision of Theodor Herzl, the inhabitants of the 'state of the Jews' would speak his language, German; however, the Zionist colonists who had previously expressed themselves in Yiddish did not view kindly the refugees from Germany who arrived in the wake of the advent of Nazism and the closing of the US frontiers. Indeed, those refugees were commonly perceived as 'assimilated Jews', trying at any price to import German culture to the land of the Bible – an accusation that was not totally false. The contemptuous view that the Ashkenazim (the old term for the refined Jews of Germany) had of the *Ostjuden*, as they pejoratively called the Jews of Eastern Europe, underwent a complete reversal within the Zionist enterprise: it was the descendants of these 'Orientals' who would become the dominant political élite, while also proclaiming a generalized and demonstrative disdain for the *Yekes* (German Jews).

Former Yiddish speakers were now quite happy to adopt the prestigious descriptor 'Ashkenazi', just as in antiquity the Jewish authors of the Bible appropriated 'Israel', the prestigious name of the kingdom in the north of Canaan, to denote the 'chosen people'. In this way, they wove a myth according to which their historical origin went back to civilized Germany, rather than to an East viewed as backward; in the young State of Israel, the role of inferior Oriental devolved on another population, mostly new and immigrant, who came from the West – that is, from the Maghreb.

Following the First Arab–Israeli War in 1948 and the creation of Zionist sovereignty, masses of destitute immigrants arrived from the Arab and Muslim countries that they were forced to leave. The war in Palestine was the immediate trigger of this exodus. Anti-colonial nationalism in the Arab world appeared incapable of distinguishing between religious community and secular state, thereby generating suspicion and fear, and thus contributing to this uprooting and abandonment. It was largely a tragic and painful emigration: populations from impoverished social strata in the Maghreb countries arrived in Israel, while the majority of their middle and upper-class compatriots found refuge in Europe and North America.[1] Iraqi émigrés as a group, on the other hand, while of a more heterogeneous social composition, equally experienced discrimination and much humiliation, despite the presence within their ranks of a middle class and many scholars.

The first Zionist colonists, in the late nineteenth and early twentieth centuries, had shown a certain romantic empathy with Middle Eastern folklore, but an iron wall was quickly built, behind which the Zionist community dug in so as to avoid any amalgam with Arab civilization. Relations with the indigenous culture were ultimately shaped in accordance with the tendencies of the Western Orientalism in vogue during the colonial era. In his time, Theodor Herzl already saw the future Jewish state vis-à-vis Asia as 'the advance post of civilization against barbarism', an ideological view that would be more or less shared by all the leaders of the Zionist enterprise. This lies at the root of the relationship, composed equally of blindness and severity, with the indigenous villagers who had lived on these lands for many centuries. As is well known, a large proportion of the Palestinian Arabs were uprooted and expelled during the 1948 war. Those who remained after the establishment of the Israeli state were kept under a regime of military administration for seventeen years and viewed as a lower stratum, outside the new society.

1. The Jews of Algeria were French citizens, so that very few of them emigrated to Israel after the winning of Algerian independence in 1962.

44

The Arab–Jewish immigrants, for the most part, spoke Arabic and had an Arabic (or, in some cases, Berber or Persian) everyday culture, and the Israeli authorities and institutions viewed them with varying degrees of deep contempt and manifest suspicion. David Ben-Gurion let slip on one occasion that he did not want a Moroccan culture in Israel, and that unfortunately 'the Moroccan Jews have taken much from the Moroccan Arabs'. The majority of these 'Oriental' immigrants were settled on the margins of the country and received only a minor share of the territorial booty conquered in 1949. Many Eastern European Jews, former Yiddish speakers, scarcely considered them Jews, if at all.

Ironically, these Arabic Jews had in fact remained more Jewish than had other groups of immigrants who arrived in the new state. The majority of those of Yiddish origin were more secular; accordingly, to consolidate their specific identity, they more or less consciously resorted to a mixture of traditional Jewishness and secular Yiddish ways of life that had formerly distinguished them from their non-Jewish surroundings. For the Arab-Jewish immigrants, by contrast, their religious practices were the sole markers of their Jewishness. In other words, everything that was secular and everyday in their way of life was Arabic, and consequently was the object of negative perception, if not outright rejection, on the part of the new Israeli culture that was in the process of construction.[2] Thus, for the Arabic Jews to avoid being seen as Arab within the 'Jewish state', it became necessary for them to preserve and exteriorize traditions of worship and religious ceremonies to the maximum degree.

This repression – the dissimulation and self-negation of all Arabness – greatly facilitated the lasting repression of its outward signs and its reproduction. Even though the Zionist

---

2. A further irony of history is that Maimonides, like other Jewish authors of the Middle Ages, wrote mainly in Arabic.

enterprise was fundamentally secular, the cultural schizophrenia of the Jewish Arabs did not significantly help slow the process of their secularization. It also had the effect of orienting many of them to anti-Arab positions, hence leading them to support the Zionist right, which was traditionally firmer in its hostility towards the indigenous population.

Cultural distinction, as a key phenomenon in the identity policy of social groups, is a well-known expression of modern sociology that has been well analysed by, for example, Pierre Bourdieu. It was not specific to Israel that Jewish Arabs and their descendants distanced themselves from the residues of their culture of origin. A similar phenomenon, *mutatis mutandis*, occurred among Maghrebis of Jewish origin who emigrated to France or Canada. The pressing desire not to be identified as Arab led many of their number to embrace strongly anti-Oriental political tendencies, resulting in repercussions down to the second and third generations.

Rapid Israelization certainly obscured a good part of the imported cultural differences, but on the other hand it also shored up various hierarchies established in the course of the creation of the state.

CHAPTER 7

Empty Cart, Full Cart

In 1952 the Israeli prime minister, David Ben-Gurion, met with Rabbi Avraham Yeshayahu Karelitz, known as Hazon Ish ('man of vision'). This historic encounter remained engraved in Israeli annals as a friendly 'dialogue of the deaf'. The leader of the 'Jewish state' asked the head of the 'God-fearing' Orthodox how religious and secular could live together in harmony under the new political regime. The wise rabbi, who was no Zionist and in no way viewed Israel as a Jewish state, cited the example of the camel in the Tractate Sanhedrin of the Babylonian Talmud, replying that, logically, in a narrow passage, the empty cart must give way to the full cart: secular Zionism was a hollow culture, whereas Judaism was heavily loaded. Annoyed, Ben-Gurion asked whether the commands to colonize the country, work its land and protect its frontiers did not amount in the eyes of the rabbi to a mission of Jewish culture, adding that, moreover, the secular were a majority of the Israeli population and controlled the state. The rabbi replied that for those ready to give their life for the divine commands, the opinion of the majority and the acts of the sovereign were without interest.

With the passage of time, there is no doubt that Hazon Ish was right. In comparison with the full cart of the Jewish religion, that of secular Judeity was empty and has remained so. The deeper one digs into this question, the more one is forced to recognize that there is no Jewish cultural baggage that is not religious. This is one of the main reasons for the deep contradictions of Zionism and its unswerving obsequiousness towards history, as against the world of genuine tradition.

Yet this subtle rabbi was as yet unable to perceive, in 1952, that the Zionist enterprise was in the process of creating a full cart of specifically Israeli culture, the existence of which Zionism itself had difficulty recognizing. Arbitrarily and against all logic, this creation persists in calling itself 'secular Jewish culture', despite the fact that it is not shared by the persons in other countries whom it considers Jews, whereas there is no doubt that many believers the world over share the Jewish culture of Hazon Ish.

The foundations on which the State of Israel was created were essentially laid by socialists from the various Eastern European nations. These individuals were secularists who rebelled against Judaism, yet they were forced nonetheless to adopt from the start key markers of the religious tradition, including the Jewish communitarian ethic intrinsic to it. These markers were accepted by all currents of Zionism, on the left as well as the right. The complex causes for this ideological and conceptual phenomenon were anchored in the characteristics and objectives of Zionism, beginning in the late nineteenth century and continuing through today.

To justify colonization in Palestine, Zionism appealed above all to the Bible, which it presented as a legal property title to the land. It then proceeded to depict the past of various Jewish communities not as a dense and varied fresco of the motley groups that converted to Judaism in Asia, Europe and Africa, but rather as a linear history of a race-people, supposedly exiled by force from their native land and aspiring for two thousand years to return to it. Secular Zionism deeply internalized both the religious myth of Abrahamic descent and the Christian legend of the accursed and wandering people condemned to exile for their sins. On the basis of these two matrixes, it succeeded in fashioning the image of an ethnic group whose palpably fictional character (one need only observe the diversity of appearance of Israelis) in no way subtracted from its effectiveness.

At the same time, and without embarrassment at the contradiction, the Zionist enterprise sought to create a culture that broke completely with the 'exilic' past. From the 1940s onward, a specific form of Israeli elitism prospered in the *yishuv* (the Zionist settlement), growing stronger and becoming hegemonic in the 1950s and 1960s. What mattered now was to be Israeli or, more precisely, Hebrew, while the old Jewish tradition became the object of a thinly veiled contempt not devoid of hypocrisy.

To offer one example among others, the propensity to replace 'exilic' names by Hebrew ones flourished among the cultural élites and young people of good families. 'Hebrewization' did not apply only to surnames; new parents feverishly leafed through the Bible to find rare and vigorous first names that would contrast with supposedly outmoded Jewish names such as Moshe, Yaakov, David or Shlomo. The seemingly strange names of the Talmudic rabbis of antiquity were similarly rejected: they smelled too much of the Talmudic school, the yeshivah and the wretched *shtetl*.

Canaanite names that had never had any connection with Jewish tradition, or even names that had never been spoken by Jewish lips, exercised a particular attraction. All the Israeli leaders, like their pioneer parents before them, abandoned the surnames that Jews had adopted at the time of the first modern population censuses, with David Green passing to posterity as David Ben-Gurion and Szymon Perski becoming Shimon Peres. Similarly, Yitzhak Rabin had been born Rubitzov, Ehud Barak had been Brog, Ariel Scheinermann became Sharon, the father of Benjamin Netanyahu was born Mileikowsky, and Shaul Mofaz had been the young Shahram Mofazzakar. The old names evoked the weak Jews who had been led to concentration camps and massacred like cattle, or those who slavishly aped Islamic civilization. The point was to create a 'new man' in Israel, a muscular Hebrew full of vigour, physical as well as spiritual.

To a great extent, this Hebrew identity, forged even before the creation of the state, served equally as a mark of cultural differentiation from the mass of immigrants who formed the working classes in Israel. 'Hebrewity' was mainly a practice characteristic of the cultural, political and military élites. It set the tone in the public arena at a time when the citizens of Israel were not yet so Israeli: the majority of them, of Yiddish or Maghrebi extraction, spoke modern Hebrew only with difficulty, and the new culture was outside their reach. Some of them had been secularized in Europe, but residues of Jewish, Yiddish and Arabic tradition still constituted an every-day cultural and folkloric support in the hard conditions of immigrant life.

During this time, the élites energetically pursued the production and distribution of the new culture that had gained hegemony, as we saw above, in the political and intellectual balance of forces. In this work they held two levers in their hands, at a time when television did not yet exist: the educational system and the military apparatus (and, to a lesser extent, the press). In every school, teachers instructed their pupils to speak as Israelis and read Hebrew, and taught them the Bible as a heroic and secular story. Even before the foundation of the state, the formula 'from the Bible to the Palmach'[1] was widespread. In other words, what really mattered in history was the imagined Hebraic sovereignty in antiquity, and the real Israeli sovereignty today. Ancient heroism and contemporary boldness were the identity marks of the virile Sabra.

---

1. An acronym for *plugot machatz*, or 'shock troops', a paramilitary organization predating the foundation of the State of Israel and the Tzahal, the Israeli Defense Forces.

Sickly Judaism, which had remained passive in the midst of historical events, was of secondary importance, perceived as a shaky, narrow gangway whose purpose had been to provide a transition to national renaissance.

Compulsory military service performed an equally important educational function. In parallel with compulsory education, it was an intensive melting pot, creator of an original identity and culture. The strongest contact between the élites and the mass of immigrants took place via this hierarchical apparatus. Those who, before enrolling in the army, had spoken the repugnant foreign languages of Yiddish or Arabic with their parents, found themselves recognized, after two or three years in the Tzahal, not only as good soldiers but also as far better Israelis. They then began to teach their parents the language of the state and, in so doing, to instil them with shame for their old culture, with its lack of military vigour or national majesty. That Israel found itself in the permanent position of being a besieged fortress, and won victories in the wars of 1948, 1956, and 1967, added a lustre to Israeli identity and sanctified the cult of force along with the power of the old élites.

Israeli culture solidified with remarkable speed, a fact that must be emphasized. Whereas in other states the national culture was shaped in the course of a relatively long process, in Israel, owing to its nature as a completely immigrant society, an entirely new language and culture were established and transmitted in the space of two generations. It is true that not the whole of the population received this transmission equally; subcultures continued to exist, and still do so today, but the success of the Zionist enterprise in the cultural field, as with its achievements in agriculture and military prowess, would seem unprecedented.

In high culture, too – in the visual arts, literature, poetry, theatre and cinema – artists have produced original and valuable work. Despite the rejection and derision proclaimed towards earlier cultural traditions, contemporary Israeli culture has secretly internalized certain components of that legacy. New musical tonalities, distinct from Yiddish chants or Arab melodies, have displaced the Russian airs that stirred the hearts of the young Sabras. In all public gatherings, group singing has largely replaced the old prayers. The Israelis, long before the age of globalization, adopted clothing quite different from that of the Jews of Eastern Europe or North Africa, choosing instead to adapt their costumes to the local climate, resulting in a remarkable similarity to the colonial style widespread throughout the British Empire (one exception is the *kova tembel*, the characteristic hat of the peasant Sabra). In the everyday culture of the 1970s, Israeli/Hebrew, despite variants of pronunciation, had become the common language; cooking habits, many of which had been borrowed from the Palestinians, had been standardized; and it seemed that the national cultural enterprise had reached a conclusion.

Zionism succeeded in fashioning a new people with new characteristics and its own new language, differentiated both from ancestral Jewish practices and from the anti-national conceptions that accompanied them. This people now possessed a country, though not knowing the precise location of its frontiers, and they also possessed a uniform public culture, though not always appreciating the extent to which this culture was not Jewish.

The victories that Israeli culture and the Hebrew language had achieved were accompanied, from the mid-1970s onward, by considerable flexibility and relaxation. The various cultural components of the Jewish or Arab past had ceased to represent a threat to the mechanisms of national power and came to be viewed as inoffensive and acceptable folkloric expressions, even to be cautiously encouraged. Nostalgia for Yiddishkeit became popular and legitimate; Arabic melodies were increasingly recycled into Israeli music in the guise of 'Oriental' or 'Mediterranean' songs.

Even the genocide of the subjugated and weak European Jews (who had for a time been pleasantly referred to in Israel as 'soaps' or 'cattle for slaughter'), which had been placed on a low shelf in the hierarchy of national memory, was repositioned after the great victory of 1967 and installed in a new place of honour. The reasons for this shift in the edifice of memory, however, were more complex.

CHAPTER 8

Remembering All the Victims

In April 1944, the poet Julian Tuwim published a manifesto entitled 'We, Jews of Poland', which reads, in part:

> If I had to justify my nationality, or more precisely my national sentiment, I would say that I am Polish, and this for reasons that are very simple, almost primitive, most of them rational but some irrational, if without any 'mystical' ingredient. Being Polish is not an honour, a glory or a right.
>
> It's like breathing. I have never yet met a man who took pride in breathing. I am Polish because I was born and grew up in Poland, because I went to school and university there, because in Poland I have been happy and unhappy. Because I want to return from exile to Poland, even if I am promised the pleasures of paradise somewhere else. ...
>
> In reply to this, I hear a voice say: 'All right, if you are Polish, then why this "We, Jews..."?' And I am honoured to reply, 'Because of blood.' 'In other words, a racial doctrine?' No, not at all. Not a racial doctrine, but precisely the opposite. There are two kinds of blood, that which flows in the veins, and that which flows out from the veins.

Here Tuwim expresses what it meant to be a Jew on account of the blood spilled. Prior to the Second World War, although the poet did not deny his Jewish origin, he preferred to see himself as Polish, and felt disgust at both Zionist racists and Catholic Judeophobes, all of whom sought to deny his national identity and send him to Palestine. And though he chose to return to his native country at the end of the war, the industrialized black death that had submerged Europe led him to (re)define himself in 1944 as a Jew. He had good reason: the millions murdered because of their origin were likewise unable to leave their land or change their origin. Because of Hitler, they remained Jews forever.

I remember having read Tuwim's manifesto early in my life, when it contributed to strengthening my own Jewish awareness. But I also chose, at the same time, to adopt Ilya Ehrenburg's assertion, well after the end of the Second World War, that he would remain a Jew so long as the last anti-Semite remained on the planet. And yet, as the years have passed, and in view of the radicalization of Israeli politics, especially the shifts that have taken place in its politics of memory, my assurance in this definition of my identity has steadily eroded.

One incident, among many others, will illustrate the emergence of these rifts. During my years as a doctoral student in Paris, at the École des Hautes Études en Sciences Sociales, the decision was taken to organize a university conference, the first in France, on Nazism and extermination. Representatives of the Jewish community who took part in preparations for the conference were alarmed by the invitation extended to a Roma participant and firmly opposed her coming. After great efforts, and thanks to the intervention of the historian Pierre Vidal-Naquet, the contribution of this 'non-Jewish' researcher was authorized. This incident imbued me with a lasting feeling of discouragement. My initial reaction, however, had been that of surprise, as in the early 1980s I was still unfamiliar with the intransigent claim of Jewish exclusiveness in relation to the Nazi crime.

After several events of this kind had occurred, I often found myself – at dinners in town, lectures at the university, one-off discussions – asking the question, How many people did the Nazis murder, either in concentration and extermination camps or in the other massacres they perpetrated? The response, without exception, was six million. When I made clear that my question was the total number of people and not just the number of Jews, my respondents expressed surprise. Rarely did anyone know the answer.

Any viewer of Alain Resnais' film *Night and Fog* (1955), however, could give the answer: eleven million deaths. But this number of 'non-conventional' victims of the Second World War has been wiped from the hard disk of Western collective memory. In fact, out of a total closer to ten million than eleven, Raul Hilberg, in the 1985 edition of his authoritative *Destruction of the European Jews*, determined that there were five million Jews rather than the six million he had accounted for in the first edition of his work in 1961. But it is not this difference in numbers that is important; what matters here is to know why the total number of the murdered has completely disappeared and it is only the Jewish number that is handed down.

One of the weaknesses of Alain Resnais' otherwise very successful film lies in the fact that 'the Jews' are mentioned on only two occasions. The central story focuses on the Nazi extermination apparatus, with the victims presented being mainly political prisoners, *résistants*, and Soviet prisoners of war. Sadly, it is impossible for viewers to learn anything from this film about the nature of Nazi demonization of the Jews and their obsession with the imaginary Jew. The fact that half of the 'atypical' victims were marked by the executioners as 'Jews' assumes great importance for understanding the enterprise of hatred and extermination during the Second World War. Even if many of these 'priority' victims in no way saw themselves as Jewish, but simply French, Dutch, Polish or German, they were led to massacre after having been marked by their assassins as belonging to the Jewish race-people. The embellished dialogues on this subject in Resnais' film are thus a key weakness.

Compensating for this director's weak point with regard to the Jews, however, was his boldness in depicting the characteristic cap of a French gendarme in an internment camp. Presenting this uncomfortable reality in the 1950s, when there still existed many French people who had collaborated with the Nazi occupation, required a certain intellectual courage. Unfortunately, the scene did not get past the censor.

In 1985, just thirty years after *Night and Fog*, a long and exhausting film appeared from another French director, Claude Lanzmann. Within the film culture of the late twentieth century, *Shoah* rapidly acquired iconic status as a memorial of the Nazi genocide. Should it be held against the director that, at the time, he concealed the information that a major part of his film's financing came from companies he had set up in Switzerland to receive secret funds granted him by the Israeli government? And should we not pay too much attention to the fact that at times in this terrible tragedy the main enemies of the Jews seem to be ignorant and wretched Polish peasants rather than cultivated German Nazis? The implication that the two groups stood on the same footing and were linked in a common action amounts to an intolerable distortion of history.

It is far harder, however, to excuse the surprising fact that, in a French film lasting nine hours, no mention was made of a single train reaching Auschwitz from France. In addition, there was scarcely a reference to the relative indifference of the majority of the inhabitants of the 'city of light', including the intellectuals who killed time at the Café de Flore or Les Deux Magots while Jewish children were being taken to the Vélodrome d'Hiver in July 1942. At the end of the day, the historical responsibility of the Vichy regime is totally absent from the French cult film, a fact that clearly facilitated its construction as a recognized and appreciated site of memory, in France and throughout the Western world. Many people were happy with the idea that the death industry was organized 'over there' in the distant East, anti-Semitic and grey, among frustrated and uneducated Catholic peasants, and had nothing to do with an enlightened and refined Europe.

Moreover, as an Israeli spectator of the work of a director who defines himself as a Jew, I found it hard to accept the fact that throughout a film on memory, which pays tremendous attention to detail, the presence of victims other than Jews in this gigantic death machine goes simply unmentioned. Thus, despite the great part of the film having been made in Poland, the spectator is not informed that, in fact, five million Poles were murdered: two and a half million of Jewish origin, and two and a half million Catholics. Nor is the fact that the Auschwitz camp was originally constructed for non-Jewish Polish prisoners mentioned in *Shoah*. It is scarcely surprising, then, that an American president, Barack Obama, could quite ingenuously speak of a 'Polish extermination camp'.

Of course, the great majority of Jewish Poles were wiped from the map of Poland, incinerated or buried, whereas the majority of Polish Catholics survived the war, and of course this makes an important difference in the horrific balance sheet between the dead and the living. But if proportions are taken into account, the proportion of Roma murdered in relation to the size of their communities turns out to be very close to that of the Jews, and yet they, too, receive no mention in Lanzmann's account in *Shoah*.

Unfortunately, this French director is not the only agent of memory to effect an ethnic selection when it comes to constructing the memory of the victims; he was both preceded and followed by others. For example, the permanent and deafening silence of Elie Wiesel, an immigrant who did not remain in Israel, and won the Nobel Peace Prize for having perpetuated the exclusiveness of Jewish death while never expressing the least recognition of the death of others.

From the final quarter of the twentieth century onward, the memory of almost all victims not designated by the Nazis as Semites has disappeared. The industrialized crime has become an exclusively Jewish tragedy. Western memory of the Nazi concentration camps and exterminations has been more or less emptied of other victims: Roma, *résistants* and other opponents, Communists and socialists, Jehovah's Witnesses, Polish intellectuals, Soviet commissars and officers, and so on. With the relative exception of homosexuals, all those exterminated by the Nazis, in parallel with the systematic assassination of Jews and their descendants, have also been wiped from the hegemonic network of memory. Why has this happened, and how has the construction of this new memorization influenced the characteristics of present-day Jewish identity?

In the late 1940s and throughout the next two decades, the shameful memory of the extermination of the Jews remained on the margins of Western culture and thought. In Israel, despite the Eichmann trial, the genocide did not even figure on school curricula until 1970. The subject remained highly unpopular with Jewish institutions across the world, which tackled it only cautiously. Among the several reasons for this, I shall mention just two.

The first reason bears on the caprices of the mind's history: in the immediate aftermath of the war, the survivors of the camps did not necessarily enjoy a positive image with the broad public. According to a cruel prejudice of the time, if someone had managed to emerge alive from that hell, this was seen as having very likely been at the expense of others who had been murdered. It was well known how the Nazis, before reducing human beings to dust, bent their efforts to deprive them of any sense of human solidarity, thereby reinforcing their Darwinian philosophy and easing their consciences. In this enterprise of dehumanization, they incited prisoners against one another, encouraged thefts and laughed at physical attacks. The guards and their auxiliary kapos delighted in the absence of solidarity and the general brutishness. Furthermore, on many occasions in the 1950s, survivors of the camps accused one another of unworthy behaviour in this ignoble world. During this period it was almost impossible to interview the survivors and get them to provide oral or visual testimony of their sufferings; many were ashamed of having survived.

A second reason for this long silence bears on international politics. During the Cold War, the West mobilized strongly to reintegrate West Germany into the 'democratic' family of nations. Accordingly, given that the country's élite, aside from socialists and Communists, belonged to the generation that had adulated Hitler, it was deemed preferable to prettify this past and supply a carefully doctored version. Many American films of this time presented a laundered and normalized picture of the Wehrmacht; many books were devoted to the German resistance against the Nazis and the clandestine sympathy it enjoyed. Those who 'irresponsibly' dared to infringe the rules of this cynical and selective game of memory were found primarily among the writers and artists of the political left.

From the late 1960s onward, awareness of the absolute horror slowly began to evolve. The Cold War acquired a new tone, and the Federal Republic of Germany, after paying large sums of money to Israel and compensating survivors, was now well integrated into Western political culture and the military apparatus of NATO. Israel also became, in the same period, a full and faithful partner of the Atlantic alliance and of the United States in the Middle East.

The 1967 war also played a role in this turning-point. The so-called lightning victory of the Tzahal wiped out the 'shame' that had afflicted Israeli élites since the foundation of the state. If the 'cattle' that went to slaughter had previously served as an anti-model for the formation of the nascent

Sabra, the strategy of representation of past destruction would now undergo a metamorphosis.

Israel had become a power – a small one, to be sure, but strong nonetheless, and one that dominated another people on whom it imposed an extended and brutal military occupation. The Jewish victim, yesterday hidden on account of his or her weakness, now culminated in the Jewish martyr. Acts of heroism and resistance were somewhat played down in the stories now told, leaving the most prominent place in the historical massacre to the murdered Jews, who could in no way be placed on the same level as the victims of other crimes in history.

The marginal position that the Judeocide had occupied until then in the memory of Judeo-Christian civilization was clearly intolerable, and it was important on the moral level for it to be recognized as a key element in Europe's involvement in the Second World War. To be sure, this mattered far more for Zionist and pseudo-Jewish politics. It was not enough that the memory of the victims should be engraved in the consciousness of the West. What was demanded was the specificity, exclusiveness, and total national ownership of suffering. This is the point at which we see the beginnings of what has been named the Holocaust industry, with the objective of maximizing the painful past in order to accumulate capital, not just economic, but also in terms of prestige.

All other victims were therefore dismissed, and the genocide became an exclusively Jewish matter. Any comparison with the extermination of another people was now forbidden. That is why, when Armenian descendants in the United States demanded a day of recognition to commemorate the massacre committed by the Turks, the pro-Zionist lobby joined with the latter in an attempt to block the demand. All past and present crimes were necessarily minuscule in the face of the gigantic massacre of Jews during the Second World War. Besides, from now on, those who were victims 'because they were born Jews' ceased to resemble other victims; the individuals we see in Steven Spielberg's *Schindler's List* or Claude Lanzmann's *Shoah* are victims of a special kind.

Hitler's desire to exclude Jews from the ranks of ordinary humanity has found a perverse form of expression in the memorial policy adopted by Israel and its supporters across the Western world; Zionist rhetoric, in fact, has increasingly insisted on the eternal specificity of the victim rather than that of the executioner, of the Jew and not of the Nazi. In other words, there are hosts of murderers like Hitler, while there have never been and never will be victims like the Jews. Gamal Abdel Nasser was the first to be called the 'new Hitler', before being replaced by the Palestinian Yasser Arafat and the Iraqi Saddam Hussein; most recently, the role fell to the Iranian Mahmoud Ahmadinejad. In this view of the world, and this construction of memory, the singularity of the European continent's history, from the Enlightenment on, does not lead to the Nazi organizers of the death industry but solely to the dead and persecuted of Jewish origin.[1]

The camp that comprises descendants of the survivors of extermination has steadily grown since the 1970s: nowadays, everyone wants to be a survivor. Many Americans of Jewish origin who did not live in Europe during the Second World War and did not show any effective solidarity with the victims at the time of massacre have declared themselves to be direct heirs of the survivors of the work of death. Children of Jews from Iraq and North Africa have come to view themselves

---

1. I refer to the European continent, as the two other supreme horrors of the modern age, subsequent to the Enlightenment – colonialism and Stalinism – essentially took place outside Europe. It strikes me, in fact, that the exceptional people, in the times of persecution and crime, were the 'just', who risked their lives to save others. As always in history, they were not numerous.

as an integral part of the growing community of victims of Nazism. In Israel the formula of a 'second generation' of the Shoah began to appear in the 1970s, now followed by a 'third generation'; thus, like any other capital, the symbolic capital of past suffering can be bequeathed.

The old religious identity of the 'chosen people' has gradually given way to the modern, and very effective, secular cult not only of the 'chosen victim' but also of the 'exclusive victim'. This identitarian axis of 'secular Jewishness', in its ethnocentric moral dimension, constitutes a major component enabling many to mark their self-identification as Jews, a point to which I shall return below. It has also contributed to my own growing malaise in continuing to define myself as a secular Jew, though other factors have of course also played a part.

CHAPTER 9

A Rest After Killing a Turk

A well-known Yiddish comic tale, full of self-derision, lambasts the intragroup character of Jewish morality. A Jewish mother accompanies her son to his enlistment in the tsarist army at the time of the Crimean War. At the moment of leaving him in the recruitment office, she slips a few sandwiches into his knapsack and whispers into his ear, 'Kill a Turk, and then don't forget to sit down and eat.' 'Yes, Mum,' replies the son. 'And make sure', the mother adds, 'that you rest properly after each attack when you kill a Turk.' 'Sure,' says the new recruit, and then asks, after a few seconds' hesitation, 'And what if the Turk kills me?' The mother gapes at her son and says, 'And why should he kill you? You've not done anything to him!'

During Passover in 1999, when I spent some time in San Francisco with distant relatives who were descendants of Yiddish people and who had invited me for a Pesach Seder, something strange happened to me. The majority of the guests were speakers of English, and it fell to me to recite from the Haggadah, the story of the exodus from Egypt – something which I had always abstained from doing – and then to translate the text aloud for the benefit of the Americans. This is a customary way of arousing children's interest for the traditional Passover Seder: the Haggadah is designed to educate them and transmit to them a sum of Jewish 'memories'. I took my role of instructor seriously, showing proof of creativity and emphasizing the message of liberty in the historic stories. There was a joyful ambience at that Seder, amid the recitation of the severe plagues visited upon Egypt and, as well, the consumption of fine wines.

On the way home, in the dark of the car, my daughter, then five years old, kept asking questions about the ten plagues that God had sent the wicked Egyptians. With the first plague, did the blood flow from taps or just in the rivers? Did they really drink it? What exactly did the frogs do to the people? Were the flies small or big? And so on. Even though she was half asleep, the child continued through to the tenth plague, the most disturbing in the tale of the Exodus from Egypt. What exactly did 'the first-born' mean? Did it include just boys, or were girls killed as well? When I assured her that only boys were singled out, it had a calming effect on her, and her subsequent silence persuaded me that she'd gone to sleep. But suddenly there came a final 'shock' question from the back seat: 'Did God also kill the little babies, if they were the first boy in the family?'

I remember having delayed my reply, quite embarrassed. I wasn't going to spell out to my daughter that this passage referred only to the inhabitants of Egypt, not to 'our' children: I had never been a blind and blinkered ethnocentrist. Nor did I try to invoke the pretext of 'justified' vengeance, as I found it hard to believe that even Satan himself would have invented a revenge expressed in the deliberate killing of young children. Nor could I tell her that this was an objective description of a divine action that passes our understanding. What did she know, after all, about objectivity and neutrality? And just a couple of hours earlier, she had listened to the powerful chant in which we thanked God for the plague on the first-born, and had herself murmured, after me, 'That suffices for us.'

I racked my brains to find other ways of not quite replying in case the questioning resumed the next morning, but I was blocked by a paralysing apprehension. What would happen if she wanted us to read the Haggadah again, and we reached the supplication for vengeance, addressed to God: 'Pour down Your wrath on the peoples that do not know thee ... and destroy them from under Your heaven'?

The compilation known as the Haggadah has long occupied a key place in Jewish cultural life. The first known version dates from the ninth century. We are unsure exactly when the explicit demand to exterminate all the peoples who did not believe in the God of the Jews and had dared to attack Israel was inserted. We do know for certain, however, that in the Middle Ages, Judeophobic priests were familiar with this text and made use of it periodically to inflame people's minds against these heretical murderers of Jesus, condemning them to revenge by spreading atrocious accusations of ritual crimes. It is also well known that an inflammatory connection between infant blood and *matzo* (the unleavened bread of Passover) was used as a popular weapon by a number of provocateurs.

I suppose that my two grandmothers and my grandfather still celebrated the Pesach Seder while they were imprisoned in the Lodz ghetto, before being asphyxiated in lorries designed to achieve that effect but which did not function very well and were thus soon replaced by the more effective gas chambers. I do not know whether, in their Passover prayers, my grandparents arrived at that terrifying sentence calling for wrath and destruction, but I am sure that the world today would be full of indulgence for them, as I am indeed myself. It is understandable that the weak and persecuted should cry vengeance without having to justify every one of their acts and every word they speak. But what attitude should we adopt towards the 'secular Jewish' intellectuals in Paris, London or New York who in our own day read the Haggadah with enthusiasm and self-satisfaction, while not eliminating from it the outrages against the *goyim*? And a still more thorny question: How should we view the fact that this unfortunate sentence is pronounced by the Israeli pilots who rule the skies of the Middle East, or by armed columns that patrol alongside defenceless Arab villages in the occupied West Bank?

Many people, deprived of the consoling belief in God, newly identify as secular Jews and today invoke the excellence of Jewish ethics. For some time now, many intellectuals have sought to credit Judaism with a superior ethic of love for the Other and immanent solidarity with the suffering and oppressed. Yet for centuries Jews were stigmatized for their moral degradation as unscrupulous usurers or swindling merchants (the portrayals in Shakespeare or Dickens are not exceptional). Of course, it was not the Talmud that led Jews to concentrate on 'shameful' activities such as moneylending, dealing in gold, or hawking; these fields were most commonly forced on them by the Christian world, which denied them the right to own property or work the land. Once transformed into wretched swindlers, insult was added to injury, attributing to Jews essentialist traits induced, not by their activities, but by an inborn greed fuelled by their beliefs. The descendants of Judas Iscariot, having rejected the grace of Jesus, could subsist only as parasites living on dirty money. Was this not what the Talmud laid down? Was this not always their historic destiny?

Charles Fourier and Pierre-Joseph Proudhon were not alone in the sacrifice to historical stupidity that consists of characterizing Judaism as worship of a money God: the young Karl Marx himself slipped in that direction for a while. The fact that Jews and their descendants distinguished themselves as bankers and businessmen was indeed not due to chance, but the causes of this phenomenon are socio-historical, not ideological. The latter explanation was attempted by Werner Sombart, but he went astray in several of his hypotheses.

In the second half of the twentieth century, in the wake of the shockwave of genocide, anti-Jewish views gradually underwent a radical change. Various intellectual circles focused on the undeniable fact that many sons and daughters of the Jewish bourgeoisie did not follow the ancestral path of capital accumulation but, on the contrary, took a stand on the side of the oppressed and exploited. From Karl Marx himself, who devoted his life to the industrial proletariat of the nineteenth century, to Leon Trotsky and Rosa Luxemburg in the early years of the twentieth century, Léon Blum in the 1930s, through to Howard Zinn and the hundreds of young people involved in the struggle for the equal rights of blacks in the United States or in support of the Vietnamese, there were many scions of Jewish families who rebelled and consistently fought for the advent of justice and social rights.

The image of the Jews thus underwent a positive turn, culminating in the philo-Semitic, 'Judeo-Christian' Europe of today. Now it has become a habit to seek an immanent causality for the massive presence of Jewish descendants who have taken the side of culture and progress. Many people have hastened to perceive this as the imprint of a deep-rooted Jewish morality. The motivations for the widespread revolt against injustice have been explained in terms of the Jewish education received from parents, seemingly based on a long-standing humanist tradition. According to this approach, the 'people' that gave the world the Ten Commandments continued their particular trajectory among other nations to initiate them in the sublime principles of the biblical prophets. It has now been deemed useful to cite, for example, Martin Buber's religious philosophy of dialogue or, more recently, the theory of the Other in the philosophical work of Emmanuel Levinas.

However, just as the ill repute of Jews in the past was based on fundamentally untrue assertions, so too is the image of Jewish moral superiority put forward today no more than a myth, cobbled together and lacking historical foundation – a fact that neither the thinking of Buber nor Levinas can refute.

Jewish tradition has essentially been based on an intragroup ethos. Other religious communities as well exhibit the lack of a universalistic ethics, but in the Jewish case this is more visible, strongly reinforced by the Jews' isolation and self-withdrawal as a result of the persecutions they underwent. For a span of several centuries, Judaism continued to fashion a strongly particularist ethnoreligious morality.

It is customary, to demonstrate the universalistic foundation of Judaism, to cite Leviticus 19:33–34: 'When an alien settles with you in your land, you shall not oppress him. He shall be treated as a native born among you, and you shall love him as a man like yourself, because you were aliens in Egypt. I am the Lord'. The term 'alien' here (*Ger*, in Hebrew) should be seen as meaning 'new inhabitant', but it is likely that it refers exclusively to immigrants who adopted the belief in Yahweh as per the biblical commandments. The Bible expressly forbids coexistence between idolaters and the followers of Yahweh on the divinely promised land, which is why '*Ger*' is never applied to Canaanites or to uncircumcised Philistines.

The famous aphorism 'You shall love your neighbour as yourself' (Leviticus 19:18), repeated by Jesus in the New Testament (Matthew 19:19, Mark 12:31, Romans 13:9), is indeed a biblical teaching. But few are prepared to recognize that the complete verse in Yahweh's sacred text begins thus: 'You shall not seek revenge, or bear any grudge against the sons of your own people, but you shall love your neighbour as yourself.' That is why Maimonides, the greatest Jewish exegete of all time, in his *Mishneh Torah*, interpreted the phrase as follows: 'Every man should love all those of Israel like himself ...' For Yahwism, as for subsequent Judaism, there was no doubt that this principle concerned only those who shared the same faith, not the whole of humanity.

Viewers of Steven Spielberg's moving film *Schindler's List*, with its accolade of Oscars, will have heard at the end the noble and generous declaration about the German who rescued Jews: 'He who saves a single life has preserved a whole world.' How many know that in the Babylonian Talmud, which has always been the determining text for Jewish law, it is written: 'He who saves a single life in Israel ... has saved a whole world' (Tractate Sanhedrin 5, Mishnah 4). Spielberg's cosmetic rhetoric proceeded from praiseworthy intentions and pleased many, but the Hollywood-style humanism of the film has little to do with Jewish tradition.

As we know, throughout the centuries Jews studied the Talmud far more than the Bible. True, the Pentateuch was well known in the Talmudic schools, thanks to the *Parashat Hashavoua* (the weekly extract from the Torah read in public every Shabbat), but there was no debate or argument about the messages of the great prophets. It was the Christian tradition, more than the Jewish, that became imbued with the universalistic aspects of the biblical prophecy. The position of inequality towards the non-Jewish Other, however, was not always as unambiguous as in the Talmud: 'You shall be called men, but the idolaters are not called men' (Tractate Yebamoth 61a). And it was not the work of chance, for example, that Avraham Yitzhak HaCohen Kook, the main architect of the process of nationalization of the Jewish religion in the twentieth century, and first Ashkenazi chief rabbi of the colonist community in Palestine before the founding of the State of Israel, was able to write, in his book *Orot* (Enlightenment):

> The difference between a soul of Israel, with its authenticity, its inner desires, its aspirations, its quality and its vision, and the soul of all non-Jews, is greater and deeper at all levels than the difference between the soul of a man and that of an animal; among the latter there is only a quantitative difference, whereas between these and the former there is a qualitative difference in kind.

It is important to know that the writings of Rabbi Kook are still used today as a spiritual guide for the community of religious–national settlers who have established themselves in the occupied territories.

This leads us to a comparison. The moral principles of the Ten Commandments presented in the Bible have, in the West, become the common legacy of believers in a single God. They appeared for the first time in the mythological context of a place on Mount Sinai, and were consecrated by all three Western religions: Judaism, Christianity and Islam, considered the foundation of monotheism as a universalistic faith. But should they be seen as the universal ethical basis of Judaism?

In the same striking mythological place where he appeared to the Hebrew prophet Moses, God also undertook to exterminate all the inhabitants of Canaan in order to make room in the Promised Land for the sons of Israel. So, just three short chapters in the Bible after the Ten Commandments, including the declaration 'Thou shall not kill', a mass murder was promised: 'My angel will go before you and bring you to the Amorites, the Hittites, the Perizzites, the Canaanites, the Hivites, and the Jebusites, and I will make an end of them' (Exodus 23:23). In the course of history, the Jews became familiar with this promise and its cruel expression in the continuation of the story; as consistent believers, they were constrained to accept and sanctify a divine law whose logic could not be challenged.

This genocidal Yahwistic tradition was transmitted, along with the Ten Commandments, to the two other monotheistic faiths, permitting or even encouraging them to eliminate idolaters who stubbornly refused to recognize the superiority of a single omnipotent God. It was not until the eighteenth century, and the Enlightenment, that a criticism of these terrible prescriptions was formulated, and a distance taken. That was the doing of Jean Meslier, Thomas Chubb, Voltaire and other philosophers, who made clear the anti-universalistic religious morality characteristic of the Bible, on which were nourished, indirectly, all those Jews, Christians and Muslims who revered the sacred text as a living God.

It took great effort for Jewish descendants, in the course of secularization, to break from this egocentric ethical tradition and join in a broader, universalistic morality. Though some were aware that the dream would never be fully realized, they had to believe in and adhere to the modern principles of liberty, equality and fraternity that were deemed to have become the common aspiration of humanity. Without the upheavals induced by the age of Enlightenment, without the universal conception of the rights of man and of the citizen, and then of social rights, we would never have seen the emergence of intellectuals and leaders such as Karl Marx, Leon Trotsky, Rosa Luxemburg, Kurt Eisner, Carlo Rosselli, Léon Blum, Otto Bauer, Pierre Mendès-France, Abraham Sarfati, Daniel Cohn-Bendit, Noam Chomsky, Daniel Bensaïd, Naomi Klein, and a good many others, close or distant heirs of a Jewish background.

The distancing of these individuals, and so many more, from the Jewish religious tradition was inversely proportional to their convergence with a humanist view of the world and a burning desire to change the conditions of people's lives, whoever those people might be, and not just members of their own religion, their own community or their own nation. This problematic requires further clarification and exploration: Was it mere chance that the domains of revolution, protest, reform and utopia attracted so many individuals whose origins go back to a Jewish past?

The oppression exercised by the dominant religious civilizations towards a religious minority prepared the ground so that, with the advent of the Enlightenment, a section of the oppressed joined, in the course of their secularization, with all those who suffered, proclaiming solidarity with them. Modern Judeophobia, moreover – which persists in seeing such individuals as Jews despite their clearly expressed desire – strengthened the frequent aspiration to a universal morality: to liberate ourselves, the whole world must be liberated; to obtain our own liberty, all persons must be free, on principle.

A residue of the messianic tradition of hope, the foundation of the ancestral Jewish faith, may have continued to echo among some of these individuals, though it is hard to find confirmation of this. Jewish sensibility was imbued with a burning desire for religious salvation, which, in the wake of alienation, persecution, and secularization, became translated into a keen desire for deliverance through revolution and for the attainment of a more just world, synonymous with the end of history, the end of suffering, the end of oppression.

For several generations subsequent to the beginnings of emancipation, while the winds of Judeophobia continued to blow, many descendants of Jews filled the battalions of those who challenged the established order. They became nonconformists par excellence in modern times. But this of course was not true of all Jews, a majority of whom, along with their secularized descendants, preferred to support the established powers. Nevertheless, there were a large number of rebel intellectuals whose parents issued from the Jewish cultural world – a development not at all to the liking of conservatives or the Judeophobic right.

With the disappearance of political anti-Semitism and the devalorizing of utopia in the Western spiritual universe, that phenomenon underwent rapid changes. As revolutionary universalism lost prestige in the wake of revelations of the atrocious crimes committed by Communist regimes, this was sadly accompanied by a dissolution of the principles of general human solidarity, even if other factors were also involved. The ranks of intellectuals inspired by a universalistic consciousness – sons or daughters of immigrant Jews, ready to stand always on the side of the persecuted – have singularly declined; a large fraction even proclaim themselves increasingly conservative. Some seek a return to Jewish religious tradition, whereas others, a greater number, have become enthusiastic defenders of all Israeli policies and actions in the Middle East.

Anyone who seeks to establish a connection between Jewish morality and social justice, between Jewish tradition and human rights, must ask why the Jewish religious sphere has barely given rise to preachings against repeated Israeli attacks on human rights. In our own day, still, hardly any protests are forthcoming from Jewish institutions against the grave injustices committed under the Israeli occupation. A few young rabbis here and there show signs of compassion towards the distress of others, but they are the exception, while the solidly organized Jewish communities have never mobilized in support of persecuted non-Jews. Talmudic students, full of energy, have never turned to protests against the oppression experienced by others: such initiatives would go completely against the traditional religious mentality.

At the same time, it is imperative that we avoid confusion and not equate Judaism with Zionism. Judaism firmly opposed Jewish nationalism until the twentieth century, and even until the arrival of Hitler. Jewish organizations and institutions, with the massive support of their members, rejected the idea of colonization of the Holy Land and, *a fortiori*, the creation of a state that would be 'the Jewish state'. It must be made clear that this consistent opposition did not result from a humanist identification with the local inhabitants who were steadily being uprooted from their land. In their firm opposition to Zionism, the great rabbis were not guided by universal moral imperatives. Rather, they quite simply understood that Zionism represented, in the end, a collective assimilation into modernity, and that worship of the national soil, expressed in a new secular faith, would supplant devotion to the divine.

The creation of the State of Israel, its military triumphs and its territorial expansion, eventually carried along the great majority of the religious camp, which underwent an accelerated radical nationalization. Large blocs of religious nationalists and nationalist Orthodox are today among the most ethnocentric elements of Israeli society. They were not led down this path by the Bible or the Talmud, and yet the main messages of the holy book and its commentators did not guard them against a slippage into brutal racism, a frenetic desire for territory, and a crying failure to take into consideration the native inhabitants of Palestine.

In other words, perhaps the egocentric dimensions that characterize traditional Jewish morality do not bear direct responsibility for the anti-liberal and anti-democratic collapse that we are witnessing today in Israel; however, they have incontestably made it possible and continue to authorize it. When a tradition of intragroup ethics is combined with a religious power, a national power, or a party, it invariably generates terrible injustices against those who are excluded, who are viewed as not part of the community.

CHAPTER 10

Who Is a Jew in Israel?

In 2011, at Ben Gurion Airport outside Tel Aviv, I was preparing to catch a flight for London. The security inspection took a long time, and passengers were showing signs of impatience. Like everyone else, I was tired. Suddenly my gaze was drawn to a woman sitting on a bench near the check-in desk; her head, though not her face, was covered by the traditional scarf (misnamed a 'veil' by Western media). She was being guarded by two Israeli security agents, who had taken her from the queue a few moments before. It was not hard to figure out that she was a 'non-Jewish' Israeli. Around me, the Jewish Israelis seemed not to see her, as if she were completely transparent.

It was a routine embarkation scene. Israeli Palestinians are always separated from the rest of the passengers before being subjected to a special questioning and search. The justification given, and considered self-explanatory, is fear of a terrorist attack. The fact that Israeli Arabs have not been involved in such attacks, and that terrorism has declined in the past few years, has not led to the relaxation of surveillance. In the national state of Jewish immigrants, indigenous Palestinians remain suspect, and are to be permanently watched.

I felt ill at ease, and made a gesture of impotence towards her. She examined me for a moment in a questioning silence. Her look did not exactly correspond to the description given by my father of the look in the eyes of a Jew, but it, too, expressed sadness, the experience of offence, and profound fear. Suddenly she smiled at me, and her expression became one of resignation. A few minutes later, I reached the check-in desk and passed through without the slightest difficulty. I was almost ashamed, and did not dare to turn my head in her direction. In writing these lines, I am turning my head towards her now. That fleeting encounter brought home to me that in Israel, being a Jew means, fundamentally and before all else, not being an Arab.

Since the founding of the State of Israel, secular Zionism has had to confront a fundamental question to which not even its supporters abroad have so far found an answer: Who is a Jew?

Talmudic Judaism did not pose this kind of question. In the Talmud, in complete contrast to the Bible, the Jew has always been someone who either is born of a Jewish mother or has converted according to the law, and upholds the essential precepts. At a time when atheism did not exist, a time when, if someone abandoned Judaism (as many did), he cleaved to another faith, it was clear that by changing religion that person ceased to be a Jew in the eyes of the community. With the advent of secularism, a Jew who stopped performing religious duties but did not opt for a different belief might arouse sadness within their family but nonetheless continued in a certain sense to be considered a Jew, because the hope remained that, so long as the person did not become Christian or Muslim, he might one day return to the bosom of the faith.

In the first years of existence of the State of Israel, although waves of immigration brought their share of 'mixed couples', Zionism tried not to pay attention to this problem, but it soon became clear that the definition of a Jew based on a voluntary principle could not be preserved. Given that the 'law of return' automatically gave, to all those defined as Jews, a right to emigrate to the new state and obtain citizenship there, such an opening of the gates risked challenging and muddying the ethno-religious legitimacy of the colonization on whose principles secular Zionism was based. Besides, Zionism had confirmed a definition of Jews as a 'people' of unique origin and, as in Judaism before it, the 'assimilation' between Jews and neighbouring peoples was a development to be feared.

This is why, in the secular state being created, civil marriage was prohibited, and only religious unions were authorized and performed. Someone who is defined as a Jew may marry only a Jew, a Muslim may marry only a Muslim, and this strictly segregationist law likewise holds for the Christian and the Druze. A secular Jewish couple can adopt a non-Jewish (that is, Muslim or Christian) child only by converting him or her to Judaism in accordance with rabbinical law; the notion of a child of Jewish origin being adopted by a Muslim couple is not even envisaged. Contrary to widespread assumptions, the perpetuation of this pseudo-religious legislation is not due to the electoral weight of the religious community; it results from uncertainties bearing on secular Jewish identity, and the desire to preserve a Jewish ethnocentrism. Israel has never been a rabbinical theocracy; from birth, it has remained a Zionist ethnocracy.

This ethnocracy, however, must continually respond to a cardinal problem. Israel defines itself as a 'Jewish state', or as the 'state of the Jewish people' throughout the world, but it is not even able to define who is a Jew. The attempts made in the 1950s to identify Jews on the basis of fingerprints, like more recent experiments aimed at distinguishing a Jewish DNA, have all failed. Zionist scientists in Israel and abroad may well have proclaimed the existence of a 'genetic purity' that Jews have preserved down through the generations, but they have not managed to characterize a Jew on the basis of the DNA genotype. Nor are cultural or linguistic criteria of any use in defining Jews, given that their descendants have never shared a common language or culture. As a result, only religious criteria remain at the disposal of secular legislators: someone who is born of a Jewish mother, or has converted according

79

to religious law and regulation, is recognized by the State of Israel as a Jew, an exclusive and eternal co-proprietor of the state and the territory that it administers. Which also explains the growing need, in the official identity policy of the State of Israel, to preserve religious customs.

Besides, since the late 1970s, and increasingly so with the passage of time, emphasis has been laid on the idea that the State of Israel is Jewish, not Israeli. The first adjective, as we have seen, refers to the Jews of the whole world, whereas the second 'only' includes all citizens living in Israel: Muslims, Christians, Druze and Jews without distinction. Despite the fact that in everyday life, cultural Israelization has reached a high level of maturity (Israeli Palestinians have undergone acculturation and speak perfect Hebrew). But instead of recognizing this identity, enshrining it, and seeing it as the melting pot of an inclusive republican and democratic consciousness, the opposite has occurred, with the state becoming ever more Judeocentric.

On the one hand, we have the everyday Israeli cultural reality; on the other, a Jewish super-identity generated by Israeli identity policy through a strange schizophrenia in conflict with itself. On the one hand, the Israeli state has increasingly proclaimed that it is Jewish, and as a result is obliged to subsidize ever more cultural enterprises and traditional religious and national establishments at the expense of the teaching of general humanities and scientific knowledge. On the other hand, the old intellectual élites and a segment of the secular middle class have continued to chafe at the restrictions imposed by religious constraints. The latter have tried to act 'without' while continuing to feel 'with': they would like to remain Jews without Judaism, but fail to see the impossibility of this.

Many factors may explain the emphasized Judaization of state identity. This tendency probably results principally from the inclusion of a large Palestinian population under the direct power of Israel. The Palestinians of the apartheid zones in the occupied territories, along with the Arab citizens of Israel, represent a demographic mass that is perceived as critical and threatening to the pseudo-Jewish character of the state.

The increased need for the identity of the state to be a Jewish identity may also have its origin in the victory of the Zionist right, which benefited mainly, though not uniquely, from the support of Jews of Arab origin. That category of Jews, as we saw, had preserved their Jewish identity in a far stronger form than had members of other immigrant groups, and from 1977 on, that strength was expressed politically, in an electoral victory that has had a lasting effect on the path subsequently followed by Israel.

Starting in the late 1980s, the instrumentalized arrival of the 'Russians', with their very different characteristics, likewise contributed to the exacerbation of this general tendency. In the case of those new immigrants, it was actually the absence of any Jewish tradition or any familiarity with Israeli culture that led the Zionist institutions to emphasize a Jewishness stamped not in their specific cultural inheritance but in an essence – in other words, their DNA. This identitarian campaign was complicated by the fact that a more than negligible part of this population was not Jewish in any sense, so that many Russian immigrants only discovered their 'Jewishness' by way of a strong anti-Arab racism.

An additional explanation can be offered: the decline of classic nationalism in the Western world and the rise of communitarianism or a transnational tribalism (a subject that I shall return to below) manifested their first symptoms in Israel. What value could a minor Israeli cultural identity have in an age of globalization? Wasn't it preferable, in those historical conditions, to develop a supranational 'ethnic' identity that would, on the one hand, give the descendants of Jews across the world the feeling that Israel belonged to them, and would, on the other hand, maintain among Israeli Jews the consciousness of forming part of a great Jewish people, whose members were perceived as exercising true power in all Western capitals? Why not belong to a 'world people' that had produced so many Nobel laureates, so many scientists, so many film-makers? A local Israeli or Hebrew identity has lost much of its past prestige, and gradually given way to an insistent and hypertrophied Jewish self-identity. In this way, as we saw, certain aspects of the Jewish tradition have found a new lease on life in many of the new Jews.

A comparative example will help elucidate the identitarian laws of citizenship and education that have been conspicuously strengthened and refined in Israel since the 1980s. If the United States of America decided tomorrow that it was not the state of all American citizens, but rather the state of those persons around the whole world who identity as Anglo-Saxon Protestants, it would bear a striking resemblance to the Jewish State of Israel. African Americans, Latin Americans or Jewish Americans would still have the right to take part in elections to the House of Representatives and the Senate, but the representatives of those chambers would have to understand and make known quite clearly that the American state must remain eternally Anglo-Saxon.

To grasp this issue better, let us expand on this parallel. Imagine that in France it was suddenly decided to change the constitution and establish that the country was to be defined as a Gallo-Catholic state, and that 80 per cent of its territory could be sold only to Gallo-Catholics, despite the fact that its Protestant, Muslim or Jewish citizens would continue to enjoy the right to vote and be elected. The tribalist, anti-democratic current would soon extend across Europe. In Germany difficulties would arise, bearing on the stigmata of the past, in connection with the official rehabilitation of the earlier ethnocentric principles, yet the Bundestag would successfully overcome the obstacles and decree that foreign immigrants who had already obtained citizenship and taken part in political life could not marry Germans of Aryan Christian origin, with a view to preserving the German *ethnos* for another thousand years. Great Britain would solemnly proclaim that it no longer belonged to any of its British subjects – the Scots, the Welsh, the citizens descended from immigrants from the former colonies – but was henceforth the state only of the English, those born to an English mother. Spain would cause problems by tearing off the veil of national hypocrisy and declaring that it was no longer the property of all Spaniards but an explicitly Castilian-democratic state which generously granted its Catalan, Andalusian and Basque minorities a limited autonomy.

Were historical changes like these to become reality, Israel would finally accomplish its destiny of being a 'light among the nations'. It would feel far more at ease in the world, and clearly less isolated, in its exclusive identitarian policy. But there is a shadow in this picture: measures of this kind are unacceptable in the context of a 'normal' democratic state based on republican principles. Liberal democracy has never been solely an instrument for the regulation of relations between classes; it has also been an object of identification for all its citizens, who are supposed to believe that they have a property title to it and in this way directly express their sovereignty. The symbolically inclusive dimension has played a major role in the advent of the democratic nation-state, even if a certain gap has always persisted between symbol and reality.

A policy like that of Israel's towards its minority groups who do not belong to the dominant *ethnos* is rarely found today outside the post-Communist countries of Eastern Europe, where there exists a nationalist right wing that is significant if not hegemonic.

According to the spirit of its laws, the State of Israel belongs more to non-Israelis than it does to its citizens who live there. It claims to be the national inheritance more of the world's 'new Jews' (for instance, Paul Wolfowitz, former president of the World Bank; Michael Levy, the well-known British philanthropist and peer in the House of Lords; Dominique Strauss-Kahn, former managing director of the International Monetary Fund; Vladimir Gusinsky, the Russian media oligarch who lives in Spain) than of the 20 per cent of its citizens identified as Arabs, whose parents, grandparents and great-grandparents were born within its territory. Various nabobs of Jewish origin from around the world thus feel the right to intervene in Israeli life; through massive investment in the media and the political apparatus, they increasingly seek to influence its leaders and its orientation.

Intellectuals who know well that the state of the Jews is their own also figure among the ranks of the 'new Jews'. Bernard-Henri Lévy, Alan Dershowitz, Alexandre Adler, Howard Jacobson, David Horowitz, Henryk M. Broder and numerous other champions of Zionism, active in various fields of the mass media, are quite clear about their political preferences. Contrary to what Moscow meant for Communists abroad in former times, or Beijing for the Maoists of the 1960s, Jerusalem really is their property. They have no need to know the history or geography of the place, nor are they obligated to learn its languages (Hebrew or Arabic), to work there or pay taxes, or – thank heaven! – to serve in its army. It is enough to make a short visit to Israel, readily obtain an identity card, and acquire a secondary residence there before returning immediately to their national culture and their mother tongue, while remaining in perpetuity a co-proprietor of the Jewish state – and all this simply for having been lucky enough to be born of a Jewish mother.

The Arab inhabitants of Israel, on the other hand, if they

marry a Palestinian of the opposite sex in the occupied territories, do not have the right to bring their spouses to live
in Israel, for fear that they will become citizens and thereby
increase the number of non-Jews in the Promised Land.

That last assertion, in fact, requires a certain amplification.
If an immigrant identified as Jewish arrives from Russia or the
United States along with his non-Jewish wife, the latter will
have the right to citizenship. However, even if the spouse and
her children are never considered Jews, the fact that they are
not Arab will prevail over the fact of not being Jewish. 'White'
immigrants from Europe or America, even if not Jewish, have
always enjoyed somewhat tolerant treatment. To diminish
the demographic weight of the Arabs, it is judged better to
weaken the Jewish state through non-Jewish dilution, so long
as the newcomers are white Europeans.

At the same time, it is necessary to be aware that the state of
the Jews is not thoroughly Jewish. To be a Jew in the State of
Israel does not mean that you have to respect the commandments or believe in the God of the Jews. You are allowed, like
David Ben-Gurion, to dabble in Buddhist beliefs. You may,
like Ariel Sharon, eat locusts while keeping a kosher house-
hold. You may keep your head uncovered, as do the majority
of Israeli political and military leaders. In most Israeli towns,
public transport does not operate on the Shabbat, but you
should feel free to use your own car as much as you like. You
may gesticulate and hurl insults at a football stadium on the
sacred day of rest, and no religious politician will dare protest.
Even on Yom Kippur, the holiest day in the Jewish calendar,
children freely play on their bicycles in every courtyard in
the city. As long as they do not come from Arabs, anti-Jewish
abominations remain legitimate in the state of the Jews.

What is the meaning, then, of being 'Jewish' in the State
of Israel? There is no doubt about it: being Jewish in Israel
means, first and foremost, being a privileged citizen who

enjoys prerogatives refused to those who are not Jews, and particularly those who are Arabs. If you are a Jew, you are able to identity with the state that proclaims itself the expression of the Jewish essence. If you are a Jew, you can buy land that a non-Jewish citizen is not allowed to acquire. If you are a Jew, even if you speak only a stumbling Hebrew and envisage staying in Israel only temporarily, you can be governor of the Bank of Israel, which employs only four Israeli Arabs in subordinate positions out of a staff of seven hundred. If you are a Jew, you can be minister of foreign affairs and live permanently in a settlement located outside the legal borders of the state, alongside Palestinian neighbours deprived of all civic rights as well as of sovereignty over themselves. If you are a Jew, you can not only establish colonies on land that does not belong to you, but can also travel through Judea and Samaria on roads that the local inhabitants, living in their own country, do not have the right to use. If you are a Jew, you will not be stopped at roadblocks, you will not be tortured, you will not have your house searched in the middle of the night, you will not be targeted nor will you see your house demolished by mistake. These actions, which have continued for close to fifty years, are designed and reserved solely for Arabs.

In the State of Israel in the early twenty-first century, does it not appear that being a Jew corresponds to being a white in the southern United States in the 1950s or a French person in Algeria before 1962? Does not the status of Jews in Israel resemble that of the Afrikaners in South Africa before 1994? And is it possible that it might soon resemble the status of the Aryan in Germany in the 1930s? (Resemblance has its limits, however: I utterly reject the least comparison with Germany in the 1940s.)

How, in these conditions, can individuals who are not religious believers but are simply humanists, democrats and liberals, and endowed with a minimum of honesty, continue to define themselves as Jews? In these conditions, can the descendants of the persecuted let themselves be embraced in the tribe of new secular Jews who see Israel as their exclusive property? Is not the very fact of defining oneself as a Jew within the State of Israel an act of affiliation to a privileged caste which creates intolerable injustices around itself?

Finally, what is the meaning of being a secular Jew outside of Israel? Does the position taken by Julian Tuwim in 1944 – of that of my parents, who became refugees in Europe at the end of that year – still have any moral validity in 2013?

CHAPTER 11

Who Is a Jew in the Diaspora?

It is 2011. I am attending a discussion in a good London bookshop on the occasion of the publication of one of my books. The organizer of the evening's proceedings, a philosopher from Oxford, a charming and subtle man, introduces me with evident sympathy. He makes clear that he is, like me, a critic of Israel's militarist policy, that he is enraged by its racism, the complacency with which it presents itself as Jewish, the apartheid policy it has applied in the occupied territories, and so forth. Yet he expresses, albeit with delicacy, a reservation towards my point of view on the non-existence of a Jewish people. He feels himself part of this people, and the great majority of those attending, fairly liberal and left, indicate their agreement. In the course of the friendly exchange that follows, I ask him what constitutes the popular culture of secular Jews, and what Jewish education he can transmit to his children. He finds it hard to reply.

An elderly lady stands up and, somewhat indignant, declares that if my argument deprives her of her Jewish identity, she has nothing left. I am surprised; I seek to reassure her. It is clearly not my role to suppress people's identifications, I explain, and besides, I am certain she has many other identities as well as her Jewish one. I ask her at the same time if her liberty is also mine: do I, too, have the right to define myself as seems good to me, rather than tying myself to a painful memory that strikes me as increasingly exploited in bad faith?

Among the attendees were some individuals whom I had every reason to believe were not 'Jewish' despite being of

Middle Eastern appearance, but none of them asked to intervene in the discussion. I experienced a sense of unease: was the whole debate, which sounded 'politically correct' and manifestly non-Zionist, to be confined to an exclusive exchange reserved for 'new Jews'? Were *goyim* not supposed to take part? This question raised in me a still more complex set of problems which I had never considered until then.

Modern identity politics is packed with barbed wire, walls and roadblocks that define and limit collectives great and small. Some of these barriers can be crossed legally; others can be got round or even abolished in order to join this or that chosen group. Many social, political, national and religious circles are, in principle, open for all potential adherents. You can, for example, become an American, British, French or Israeli citizen, just as you can cease to be one. You can become an activist in a socialist movement, leader of a liberal current, or member of a conservative party; you can also resign from any one of these. All churches welcome proselytes. Anyone can become a fervent Muslim or Jew.

But how can you become a secular Jew if you are not born of parents considered to be Jews? This was the question that struck me, and that I could not manage to resolve. Is there any way of joining secular Jewry through a voluntary act, in the form of a free choice, or is this instead an exclusive, closed club whose members are selected as a function of their origin? In other words, are we not increasingly dealing with a prestigious club that, by accident though not by chance, sees itself as comprising the descendants of an ancient tribe?

Certainly, in the past, no one sought to join this closed club. No gentile envied the fate of those marked out as Jews – not in the Pale of Settlement of the Russian empire, nor in occupied Paris, nor, to be sure, in Auschwitz. Quite fortunately, however, this is no longer the case in our time, in a Western world repentant for its past persecution of Jews and desirous to expiate its sins. In the universities of New York, the studios of Hollywood, the political antechambers of Washington, in many firms on Wall Street, in the press rooms of Berlin or Paris, or in the cultural salons of London, it is rather the fashion to be a 'Jew'.

This requires no excessive effort. It is not necessary to study religion or know the history of the Jews, nor to believe in any particular god. No necessity either to learn a new language, and still less to restrain sensual and material pleasures in order to scrupulously observe the commandments. As surely as a circle is not a square, you are a Jew because you're born a Jew. And if someone is not a Jew, she cannot become one, try as she might.

In the Western world in the early twenty-first century, we are witnessing the relative decline of classic nationalism, which, two centuries after its birth, is now in poor shape. The crises of economic globalism, hand in hand with a cultural globalization disseminated by systems of communication that cross all borders, have begun to gnaw away at formerly solid national attachments. If a past era required identification with the flag and absolute fidelity to it, along with loyalty to a dominant national culture, there is now more space for partial community identities, secondary subcultures and even transnational identities, so long as they do not threaten the supreme principle of the sovereign nation-state.

Today it is far easier to express one's desire to be identified as a Jew, but the problem of 'new Jews' lies in the lack of specific cultural expressions or outward signs of the secular Jewish identity. This is why, in the United States but also elsewhere, total atheists sometimes travel to the synagogue by car on the Shabbat to have their sons circumcised (a cultural act that supposedly reduces the risk of AIDS, if we believe, oh father Abraham), and organize sumptuous Bar-Mitzvah celebrations at which the food may well not be kosher, similarly expecting to be married in due course by a rabbi, preferably a Reform rabbi, if there is one available in the local community. This, then, is how a Jew expresses his membership of this ancient and specific *ethnos* without the expenditure of any particular effort. As a result, these pseudo-religious practices, since we are not talking about people who are serious believers, have no real consequences.

The desire for an intimate context of identity, from which it would be possible to gain a certain comfort, is eminently respectable. At a time when the nation-state is increasingly unable to give meaning to large collectives, when the reserve of national enemies is exhausted and the great political and social utopias are at death's door, the renewal of community, half religious and half tribal, is capable of enhancing everyday life. And we could view with benevolent reserve the fact that, in order to maintain their Jewish identity, parents choose to have their sons circumcised, despite the fact that removal of this 'impurity' is irrational and, above all, an infringement on the fundamental right of any person to bodily integrity.

However, if in the name of maintaining an imagined Jewish identity, secular parents prevent their children from loving a partner designated as non-Jewish, afraid that they will 'marry out', this must be stigmatized as ordinary racism. 'Ethnic Jews' have good reason for concern. More than 50 per cent of Jewish American descendants marry non-Jews, and likewise in Europe. Community institutions, with the aid of the Jewish Agency, shamelessly do the maximum to restrain this tendency – well aware that, in the absence of Judeophobia, what will slowly but surely destroy the 'Jewish people' is the deep need for love and a shared life freed from the ties of tradition. Golda Meir, when prime minister of Israel, is said to have declared that the man or woman who marries a non-Jew 'adds to the six million'. She likewise proclaimed that the two dangers threatening the Jewish people were extermination and assimilation.

The ritual of commemorating the Shoah constitutes another link in the arrangements designed to preserve at all costs a separate and exclusive Jewish identity. Who could object to evoking the memory of the European horror? On the contrary, for the Western world to forget it would add insult to injury. But when Zionists and their supporters transform the memory of this destruction into a secular religion, with its cult pilgrimages to the reconstituted sites of extermination, and its aim of instilling paranoia in the consciousness of the 'Jewish' generation of tomorrow, we have to ask whether an identity constructed by the constant recall of past trauma does not generally lead to danger and trouble, both for those who are its bearers and for those who live alongside them. Despite Israel being the only nuclear power in the Middle East, it regularly reinforces terror in its supporters across the world by pointing on the future horizon to the spectre of a repeated Holocaust. Such a stance bears the ingredients of future catastrophe.

We must recognize that the key axis of a secular Jewish identity lies nowadays in perpetuating the individual's relationship to the State of Israel and in securing the individual's total support for it. If, until the 1967 war, Israel occupied a relatively secondary place in the sensibility of Jewish descendants in the West, from that point onward, this little state – which had just given a display of its great strength, even appearing as quite a power – became a source of pride for a goodly number of Jewish descendants. As is well known, any power attracts a mass of followers and comes to constitute, to a lesser or greater degree, a locus of adulation and worship. The image of soldiers of the Israel Defense Forces, svelte and spirited, perched on powerful armoured cars or leaning proudly against jet fighters, serves as an identity card for many new Jews throughout the world. The prestige that this gives has been used to the maximum by the Israeli state.

The Jewish Agency has now put an end to its final, fruitless attempts to bring 'persecuted Jews' to Israel. Since the fall of the Soviet Union, there is no longer a country in the world where the descendants of the chosen people are prevented from emigrating to the state of the Jews. Zionism has shifted the objective that originally constituted its raison d'être and acquired a second youth through a reinvigorating initiative. Now more than ever, those who aspire to identify themselves with the seed of Abraham are asked to gather funds in support of a land of the Jews that is in full territorial expansion and, above all, to activate all their networks of influence on their country's foreign policy and public opinion. The results of the latter objective have been remarkable. At a time when communitarianism enjoys growing legitimacy – particularly in an age of reverence for 'Judeo-Christian' civilization, underpinning the 'clash of civilizations' – it is more possible than ever to harbour pride at being a Jew and finding oneself on the side of the powerful who dominate history.

To be sure, a minority of individuals who define themselves as secular Jews organize protests, either individually or in a group, against the Israeli policies of segregation and occupation. They rightly see these policies as genuinely threatening the renewal of a Judeophobia that blindly and stupidly encompasses all Jewish descendants of a certain race-people and, more seriously still, confuses them with Zionists.[1] But the desire of secular Jews to continue identifying with a Jewish 'community', however understandable on the part of the generation that immediately followed the genocide, appears to be a temporary posture with little weight and no political future.

---

1. The emergence of a new Judeophobia, directly linked to the Israeli-Palestinian conflict, is regularly expressed and displayed among radical Muslims.

A particular sensibility, understandable and praiseworthy, may well be expressed among these Jewish descendants. But if those who call themselves anti-Zionist Jews without having lived in Israel and without knowing its language or having experienced its culture claim a particular right, different from that of non-Jews, to make accusations against Israel, how can one criticize overt pro-Zionists for granting themselves the privilege of actively intervening in decisions regarding the future and fate of Israel?

CHAPTER 12

Exiting an Exclusive Club

During the first half of the twentieth century, my father abandoned Talmudic school, permanently stopped going to synagogue, and regularly expressed his aversion to rabbis. At this point in my own life, in the early twenty-first century, I feel in turn a moral obligation to break definitively with tribal Judeocentrism. I am today fully conscious of having never been a genuinely secular Jew, understanding that such an imaginary characteristic lacks any specific basis or cultural perspective and that its existence is based on a hollow and ethnocentric view of the world. Earlier I mistakenly believed that the Yiddish culture of the family I grew up in was the embodiment of Jewish culture. A little later, inspired by Bernard Lazare, Mordechai Anielewicz, Marcel Rayman and Marek Edelman, I long identified as part of an oppressed and rejected minority. In the company, so to speak, of Léon Blum, Julian Tuwim and many others, I stubbornly remained a Jew who had accepted this identity on account of persecutions and murderers, crimes and their victims.

Now, having painfully become aware that I have undergone an adherence to Israel, have been assimilated by law into a fictitious *ethnos* of persecutors and their supporters, and have appeared in the world as one of the exclusive club of the elect and their acolytes, I wish to resign and cease considering myself a Jew.

Although the State of Israel is not disposed to transform my official nationality from 'Jew' to 'Israeli', I dare to hope that kindly philo-Semites, committed Zionists and exalted anti-Zionists, all of them so often nourished on essentialist conceptions, will respect my desire and cease to catalogue me as a Jew. As a matter of fact, what they think matters little to me, and still less what the remaining anti-Semitic idiots think. In the light of the historic tragedies of the twentieth century, I am determined no longer to be a small minority in an exclusive club that others have neither the possibility nor the qualifications to join.

By my refusal to be a Jew, I represent a species in the course of disappearing. I know that by insisting that only my historical past was Jewish, while my everyday present (for better or worse) is Israeli, and finally that my future and that of my children (at least the one I wish for) must be guided by universal, open and generous principles, I run counter to the dominant fashion, which is oriented towards ethnocentrism.

As a historian of the modern age, I put forward the hypothesis that the cultural distance between my great-grandson and me will be as great as, if not greater than, that separating me from my own great-grandfather. All the better! I have the misfortune of living now among too many people who believe that their descendants will resemble them in all respects, because for them peoples are eternal – *a fortiori* a race-people such as the Jews.

I am aware of living in one of the most racist societies in the Western world. Racism is most certainly present to some degree everywhere, but in Israel it exists deep within the spirit of the laws. It is taught in schools and colleges, spread in the media, and above all and most dreadful, in Israel the racists do not know what they are doing and, because of this, feel in no way obliged to apologize. This absence of a need for self-justification has made Israel a particularly prized reference point for many movements of the far right throughout the world, movements whose past history of anti-Semitism is only too well known.

To live in such a society has become increasingly intolerable to me, but I must also admit that it is no less difficult to make my home elsewhere. I am myself a part of the cultural, linguistic and even conceptual production of the Zionist enterprise, and I cannot undo this. By my everyday life and my basic culture I am an Israeli. I am not especially proud of this, just as I have no reason to take pride in being a man with brown eyes and of average height. I am often even ashamed of Israel, particularly when I witness evidence of its cruel military colonization, with its weak and defenceless victims who are not part of the 'chosen people'.

Earlier in my life I had a fleeting utopian dream that a Palestinian Israeli should feel as much at home in Tel Aviv as a Jewish American does in New York. I struggled and sought for the civil life of a Muslim Israeli in Jerusalem to be similar to that of the Jewish French person whose home is in Paris. I wanted Israeli children of Christian African immigrants to be treated as the British children of immigrants from the Indian subcontinent are in London. I hoped with all my heart that all Israeli children would be educated together in the same schools. Today I know that my dream is outrageously demanding, that my demands are exaggerated and impertinent, that the very fact of formulating them is viewed by Zionists and their supporters as an attack on the Jewish character of the State of Israel, and thus as anti-Semitism.

However, strange though this may seem, and in contrast to the locked-in character of secular Jewish identity, treating Israeli identity as politico-cultural rather than 'ethnic' does appear to offer the potential for achieving an open and inclusive identity. According to the law, in fact, it is possible to be an Israeli citizen without being a secular 'ethnic' Jew, to participate in its 'supra-culture' while preserving one's 'infra-culture', to speak the hegemonic language and cultivate in parallel another language, to maintain varied ways of life and fuse different ones together. To fully concretize and consolidate this republican political potential, it would be necessary, of course, to have long abandoned tribal hermeticism, to learn to respect the Other and welcome him or her as an equal, and to change the constitutional laws of Israel to make them compatible with democratic principles.

Most important, if it has been momentarily forgotten: Before we put forward ideas on changing Israel's identity policy, we must first free ourselves from the accursed and interminable occupation that is leading us on the road to hell. In fact, our relation to those who are second-class citizens of Israel is inextricably bound up with our relation to those who live in immense distress at the bottom of the chain of the Zionist rescue operation. That oppressed population, which has lived under the occupation for close to fifty years, deprived of political and civil rights, on land that the 'state of the Jews' considers its own, remains abandoned and ignored by international politics. I recognize today that my dream of an end to the occupation and the creation of a confederation between two republics, Israeli and Palestinian, was a chimera that underestimated the balance of forces between the two parties.

Increasingly it appears to be already too late; all seems already lost, and any serious approach to a political solution is deadlocked. Israel has grown accustomed to this, and is unable to rid itself of its colonial domination over another people. The world outside, unfortunately, does not do what is needed either. Its remorse and bad conscience prevent it from convincing Israel to withdraw to the frontiers it obtained in 1948. Nor is Israel ready to annex the occupied territories officially, as in this case it would have to grant equal citizenship to the occupied population and, by that fact alone, transform itself into a binational state. It's rather like the mythological serpent that swallowed too big a victim, but prefers to choke rather than to abandon it.

Does this mean I, too, must abandon hope? I inhabit a deep contradiction. I feel like an exile in the face of the growing Jewish ethnicization that surrounds me, while at the same time the language in which I speak, write and dream is overwhelmingly Hebrew. When I find myself abroad, I feel nostalgia for this language, the vehicle of my emotions and thoughts. When I am far from Israel, I see my street corner in Tel Aviv and look forward to the moment I can return to it. I do not go to synagogues to dissipate this nostalgia, because they pray there in a language that is not mine, and the people I meet there have absolutely no interest in understanding what being Israeli means for me. In London it is the universities and their students of both sexes, not the Talmudic schools (where there are no female students), that remind me of the campus where I work. In New York it is the Manhattan cafés, not the Brooklyn enclaves, that invite and attract me, like those of Tel Aviv. And when I visit the teeming Paris bookstores, what comes to my mind is the Hebrew book week organized each year in Israel, not the sacred literature of my ancestors.

My deep attachment to the place serves only to fuel the pessimism I feel towards it. And so I often plunge into a melancholy that is despondent about the present and fearful for the future. I am tired, and feel that the last leaves of reason are falling from our tree of political action, leaving us barren in the face of the caprices of the sleepwalking sorcerers of the tribe. But I am not a metaphysical philosopher, simply a historian who tries to compare, so I cannot allow myself to be completely fatalistic. I dare to believe that if humanity succeeded in emerging from the twentieth century without a nuclear war, everything is possible, even in the Middle East. We should remember the words of Theodor Herzl, the dreamer responsible for the fact that I am an Israeli: 'If you will it, it is no legend.'

As a scion of the persecuted who emerged from the European hell of the 1940s without having abandoned the hope of a better life, I did not receive permission from the frightened archangel of history to abdicate and despair. Which is why, in order to hasten a different tomorrow, and whatever my detractors say, I shall continue to write books like the one you have just read.